GRACE
ABOUNDING
TO THE
CHIEF OF SINNERS

John Bunyan

EVANGELICAL PRESS

P.O. Box 5, Welwyn, Herts., AL6 9NU England

Reprinted 1978 by
Evangelical Press
from the edition issued by the
American Tract Society

ISBN: 0-85234-116-4

PHOTOLITHOPRINTED BY CUSHING - MALLOY, INC.
ANN ARBOR, MICHIGAN, UNITED STATES OF AMERICA
1978

BUNYAN'S LIFE

CHAPTER I

In this my relation of the merciful working of God upon my soul, it will not be amiss if in the first place I do, in a few words, give you a hint of my pedigree and manner of bringing up; that thereby the goodness and bounty of God towards me may be the more advanced and magnified before the sons of men.

For my descent then, it was, as is well known by many, of a low and inconsiderable generation; my father's house being of that rank that is meanest and most despised of all the families in the land. Wherefore I have not here, as others, to boast of noble blood, or of any high-born state according to the flesh, though, all things considered, I magnify the heavenly Majesty, for that by this door he brought me into this world, to partake of the grace and life that is in Christ by the gospel. But yet, notwithstanding the meanness and inconsiderableness of my parents, it pleased God to put it into their hearts to put me to school, to learn me both to read and write; the which I also attained according to the rate of other men's children, though to my shame, I confess I did soon lose that little I learned, even almost utterly, and that long before the Lord did work his gracious work of conversion upon my soul.

As for my own natural life for the time that I was without God in the world, it was indeed "according to the course of this world," and "the spirit that now worketh in the children of disobedience." Eph. 2 : 2, 3. It was my delight to be taken captive by the "devil at his will," 2 Tim. 2 : 26, being filled with all unrighteousness; the which did also so strongly work and put forth itself both in my heart and life, and that from a child, that I had few equals, especially considering my years, which were tender, for cursing, swearing, lying, and blaspheming the holy name of God. Yea, so settled and rooted was I in these things, that they became as a second nature to me ; the which, as I have also with soberness considered since, did so offend the Lord, that even in my childhood he did scare and affrighten me with fearful dreams, and did terrify me with fearful visions. For often, after I had spent this and the other day in sin, I have in my bed been greatly afflicted, while asleep, with the apprehensions of devils and wicked spirits, who still, as I then thought, labored to draw me away with them, of which I could never be rid.

Also, I would at these years be greatly afflicted and troubled with the thoughts of the fearful torments of hell-fire ; still fearing that it would be my lot to be found at last among those devils and hellish fiends who are there bound down with the chains and bonds of darkness unto the judgment of the great day. These things, I say, when I was but a child but nine or ten years old, did so distress my soul, that then, in the midst of my many sports and childish vanities, amid my vain companions, I was often much cast down and afflicted in my mind therewith ; yet could I not let go my sins : yea, I was also then so overcome with despair of life and heaven, that I would often wish, either that there had been no hell, or that I had been a devil—supposing devils were

OR GRACE ABOUNDING 11

only tormentors—that if it must needs be that I went thither, I might be rather a tormentor than be tormented myself.

A while after those terrible dreams did leave me, which also I soon forgot; for my pleasures did quickly cut off the remembrance of them, as if they never had been; wherefore, with more greediness, according to the strength of nature, I still let loose the reins of my lust, and delighted in all transgressions against the law of God; so that until I came to the state of marriage, I was the very ringleader of all the youth that kept me company, in all manner of vice and ungodliness. Yea, such prevalency had the lusts and fruits of the flesh on this poor soul of mine, that, had not a miracle of precious grace prevented, I had not only perished by the stroke of eternal justice, but had also laid myself open even to the stroke of those laws which bring some to disgrace and open shame before the face of the world.

In those days the thoughts of religion were very grievous to me: I could neither endure it myself, nor that any other should ; so that when I have seen some read in those books that concerned Christian piety, it would be as it were a prison to me. Then I said unto God, "Depart from me; for I desire not the knowledge of thy ways." Job 21 : 14, 15. I was now void of all good consideration ; heaven and hell were both out of sight and mind; and as for saving and damning, they were least in my thoughts. O Lord, thou knowest my life, and my ways were not hid from thee.

But this I well remember, that though I could myself sin with the greatest delight and ease, and also take pleasure in the vileness of my companions, yet, even then, if I had at any time seen wicked things in those who professed goodness, it would make my spirit tremble. As, once above all the rest, when I was in the

height of vanity, yet hearing one swear that was reckoned for a religious man, it had so great a stroke upon
my spirit that it made my heart ache.

God did not utterly leave me, but followed me still,
not with convictions, but judgments, yet such as were
mixed with mercy. For once I fell into a creek of the
sea, and hardly escaped drowning. Another time I fell
out of a boat into Bedford river, but mercy yet preserved me alive. Besides, another time being in the field
with one of my companions, it chanced that an adder
passed over the highway; so I having a stick in my
hand, struck her over the back, and having stunned her,
I forced open her mouth with my stick, and plucked her
sting out with my fingers; by which act, had not God
been merciful unto me, I might by my desperateness
have brought myself to my end.

This also I have taken notice of, with thanksgiving:
when I was a soldier, I with others was drawn out to go
to such a place to besiege it; but when I was just ready
to go, one of the company desired to go in my room: to
which when I had consented, he took my place; and
coming to the siege, as he stood sentinel he was shot in
the head by a musket-ball, and died. Here, as I said,
were judgments and mercy, but neither of them did awaken my soul to righteousness: wherefore I sinned still,
and grew more and more rebellious against God, and
careless of my own salvation.

CHAPTER II

Presently after this I changed my condition into a married state, and my mercy was to light upon a wife whose father was counted godly. This woman and I, though we came together as poor as poor might be, not having so much household stuff as a dish or spoon between us both, yet this she had for her part, "The Plain Man's Pathway to Heaven" and "The Practice of Piety," which her father had left her when he died. In these two books I would sometimes read with her, wherein I also found some things that were somewhat pleasing to me; but all this while I met with no conviction. She also would be often telling me what a godly man her father was, and how he would reprove and correct vice, both in his house and among his neighbors; and what a strict and holy life he lived in his days, both in words and deeds.

Wherefore these books, with the relation, though they did not reach my heart to awaken it about my sad and sinful state, yet they did beget within me some desires to reform my vicious life and fall in very eagerly with the religion of the times, to wit, to go to church twice a day, and that too with the foremost; and there I would very devoutly both say and sing as others did, yet retaining my wicked life; but withal I was so overrun with the spirit of superstition that I adored, and that with great devotion, even all things, both the high-place, priest, clerk, vestment, service, and what else belonging to the church—counting all things holy that were therein contained, and especially the priest and clerk most happy, and without doubt greatly blessed, because they were the servants, as I then thought, of God, and were principal in the holy temple, to do his work therein.

_is conceit grew so strong in a little time upon my spirit, that had I but seen a priest, though never so sordid and debauched in his life, I should find my spirit fall under him, reverence him, and knit unto him; yea, I thought, for the love I did bear unto them—supposing they were the ministers of God—I could have laid down at their feet, and have been trampled upon by them, their name, their garb, and work did so intoxicate and bewitch me.

After I had been thus for some considerable time, another thought came into my mind, and that was whether we were of the Israelites or no; for finding in the Scriptures that they were once the peculiar people of God, thought I, if I were one of this race, my soul must needs be happy. Now again I found within me a great longing to be resolved about this question, but could not tell how I should; at last I asked my father of it, who told me we were not. Wherefore then I fell in my spirit as to the hopes of that, and so remained. But all this while I was not sensible of the danger and evil of sin; I was kept from considering that sin would damn me, what religion soever I followed, unless I was found in Christ: nay, I never thought of him, nor whether there was such a one or no. Thus man, while blind, doth wonder, but wearieth himself with vanity, for he knoweth not the way to the city of God. Eccles. 10 : 15.

But one day, among all the sermons our parson made, his subject was to treat of the _Sabbath-day_, and of the evil of breaking that, either with labor, sports, or otherwise. Now I was, notwithstanding my religion, one that took much delight in all manner of vice, and especially that was the day that I did solace myself therewith; wherefore I fell in my conscience under this sermon, thinking and believing that he made that sermon on purpose to show me my evil-doing. And at that time

I felt what guilt was, though never before that I can remember; but then I was for the present greatly loaded therewith, and so went home when the sermon was ended with a great burden upon my spirit.

This for that instant did benumb the sinews of my best delights, and imbitter my former pleasures to me; but behold it lasted not, for before I had well dined, the trouble began to go off my mind, and my heart returned to its old course; but Oh, how glad was I that this trouble was gone from me, and that the fire was put out, that I might sin again without control. Wherefore, when I had satisfied nature with my food, I shook the sermon out of my mind, and to my old custom of sports and gaming I returned with great delight.

But the same day, as I was in the midst of a game of cat, and having struck it one blow from the hole, just as I was about to strike it a second time, a voice did suddenly dart from heaven into my soul, which said, "Wilt thou leave thy sins and go to heaven, or have thy sins and go to hell?" At this I was put to an exceeding maze; wherefore, leaving my bat upon the ground, I looked up to heaven, and was as if I had with the eyes of my understanding seen the Lord Jesus looking down upon me, as being very hotly displeased with me, and as if he did severely threaten me with some grievous punishment for these and other ungodly practices. I had no sooner thus conceived in my mind, but suddenly this conclusion was fastened on my spirit, for the former hint did set my sins again before my face, that I had been a great and grievous sinner, and that it was now too late for me to look after heaven, for Christ would not forgive me nor pardon my transgressions. Then I fell to musing on this also; and while I was thinking of it, and fearing lest it should be so, I felt my heart sink in despair, concluding it was too late, and therefore I resolved in my mind to go on in sin; for, thought I, if the case be thus, my state is surely miserable—miserable if I leave my sins, and but miserable if I follow them: I can but be damned; and if it must be so, I had as good be damned for many sins as be damned for few.

Thus I stood in the midst of my play before all that then were present, but yet I told them nothing: but, I say, having made this conclusion, I returned desperately to my sport again; and I well remember, that presently this kind of despair did so possess my soul, that I was persuaded I could never attain to other comfort than what I should get in sin, for heaven was gone already, so that on that I must not think; wherefore I found within me great desire to take my fill of sin, still studying what sin was yet to be committed, that I might taste the sweetness of it; and I made as much haste as I could to fill my belly with its delicacies, lest I should die before I had my desires, for that I feared greatly. In these things, I protest before God I lie not, neither do I frame this sort of speech; these were really, strongly, and with all my heart, my desires. The good Lord, whose mercy is unsearchable, forgive my transgressions. And I am very confident that this temptation of the devil is more usual among poor creatures than many are aware of, even to overrun the spirits with a seared frame of heart and benumbing of conscience; which frame he stilly and slily supplieth with such despair, that though no peculiar guilt resteth upon them, yet they continually have a secret conclusion within them that there is no hope for them, for they have loved sins, therefore after them they will go. Jer. 2:25; 18:12.

Now therefore I went on in sin with great greediness of mind, still grudging that I could not be satisfied with it as I would. This continued with me about a month or more; but one day, as I was standing at a neighbor's

shop-window, and there cursing and swearing and play-
ing the madman after my wonted manner, there sat
within the woman of the house, and heard me, who,
though she was a very loose and ungodly wretch, yet
protested that I swore and cursed at that most fearful
rate that she was made to tremble to hear me ; and told
me further, that I was the ungodliest fellow for swearing
that she ever heard in all her life, and that I by thus
doing was able to spoil all the youth in the whole town,
if they came but in my company. At this reproof I was
silenced and put to secret shame, and that too, as I
thought, before the God of heaven ; wherefore while I
stood there hanging down my head, I wished with all
my heart that I might be a little child again, that my
father might learn me to speak without this wicked way
of swearing ; for, thought I, I am so accustomed to it
that it is in vain for me to think of reformation, for I
thought that could never be.

But—how it came to pass I know not—I did from
this time forward so leave my swearing that it was a
great wonder to myself to observe it ; and whereas before I knew not how to speak unless I put an oath before
and another behind to make my words have authority,
now I could without an oath speak better and with more
pleasantness than ever I could before. All this while I
knew not Jesus Christ, neither did I leave my sports and
plays. But quickly after this I fell into company with
one poor man that made profession of religion, who, as
I then thought, did talk pleasantly of the Scriptures and
of the matter of religion ; wherefore, falling into some
love and liking to what he said, I betook me to my Bible
and began to take great pleasure in reading, but especially the historical part thereof ; for as for Paul's epistles and such like scriptures I could not away with them,
being as yet ignorant both of the corruption of our na-

ture and of the want and worth of Jesus Christ to save
us : wherefore I fell to some outward reformation both
in my words and life, and did set the commandments before me for my way to heaven ; which commandments
I also did strive to keep, and as I thought did keep them
pretty well sometimes, and then I would have comfort,
yet now and then would break one, and so afflict my
conscience ; but then I would repent and say I was sorry
for it, and promise God to do better next time, and there
got help again, for then I thought I pleased God as well
as any man in England.

Thus I continued about a year, all which time our
neighbors did take me to be a very godly man, a new
and religious man, and did marvel much to see such
great and famous alteration in my life and manners ;
and indeed so it was, though I knew not Christ, nor
grace, nor faith, nor hope, for, as I have well since seen,
had I then died my state had been most fearful. But, I
say, my neighbors were amazed at this my great conversion from prodigious profaneness to something like a
moral life ; and truly so they well might, for this my
conversion was as great as for Tom of Bedlam to become
a sober man. Now therefore they began to praise, to
commend, and to speak well of me, both to my face and
behind my back. Now I was, as they said, become godly—now I was become a right honest man. But Oh,
when I understood those were their words and opinions
of me, it pleased me mighty well, for though as yet I
was nothing but a poor painted hypocrite, yet I loved to
be talked of as one that was truly godly. I was proud
of my godliness, and indeed I did all I did either to be
seen or to be well spoken of by men ; and thus I continued for about a twelvemonth or more.

CHAPTER III

Now you must know, that before this I had taken much delight in *ringing*; but my conscience beginning to be tender, I thought such a practice was but vain, and therefore forced myself to leave it, yet my mind hankered; wherefore I would go to the steeple-house and look on, though I durst not ring. But I thought this did not become religion neither, yet I forced myself, and would look on still; but quickly after I began to think, how if one of the bells should fall? Then I chose to stand under a main beam that lay overthwart the steeple from side to side, thinking here I might stand sure; but then I thought again, should the bell fall with a swing, it might first hit the wall, and then rebounding upon me, might kill me for all this beam. This made me stand in the steeple-door; and now, thought I, I am safe enough, for if the bell should fall I can slip out behind these thick walls, and so be preserved notwithstanding. So after this I would yet go to see them ring, but would not go any further than the steeple-door; but then it came into my head, how if the steeple itself should fall? And this thought—it may be for aught I know when I stood and looked on—did continually so shake my mind that I durst not stand at the steeple-door any longer, but was forced to flee for fear the steeple should fall upon my head.

Another thing was my *dancing:* I was full a year before I could quite leave that. All this while, when I thought I kept this or that command, or did by word or deed any thing I thought was good, I had great peace in my conscience, and would think with myself, God cannot choose but be now pleased with me; yea, to relate it in my own way, I thought no man in England could please God better than I. But, poor wretch as I was, I was all this while ignorant of Jesus Christ, and going about to establish my own righteousness, and had perished therein, had not God in mercy showed me more of my state by nature.

But upon a day the good providence of God called me to Bedford to work at my calling, and in one of the streets of that town I came where there were three or four poor women sitting at a door in the sun talking about the things of God : and being now willing to hear their discourse, I drew near to hear what they said, for I was now a brisk talker of myself in the matters of religion ; but I may say I heard, but understood not, for they were far above out of my reach. Their talk was about *a new birth*, the work of God in their hearts, as also how they were convinced of their miserable state by nature ; they talked how God had visited their souls with his love in the Lord Jesus, and with what words and promises they had been refreshed, comforted, and supported against the temptations of the devil ; moreover, they reasoned of the suggestions and temptations of Satan in particular, and told to each other by what means they had been afflicted, and how they were borne up under his assaults. They also discoursed of their own wretchedness of heart and of their unbelief, and did contemn, slight, and abhor their own righteousness as filthy and insufficient to do them any good.

And methought they spoke as if joy did make them speak ; they spoke with such pleasantness of scripture language, and with such appearance of grace in all they said, that they were to me as if they had found a new world—as if they were people that dwelt alone, and were not to be reckoned among their neighbors. At this I felt my own heart begin to shake and mistrust my

condition to be naught, for I saw that in all my thoughts
about religion and salvation the new birth did never
enter my mind, neither knew I the comfort of the word
and promise, nor the deceitfulness and treachery of my
own wicked heart. As for secret thoughts, I took no
notice of them, neither did I understand what Satan's
temptations were, nor how they were to be withstood
and resisted.

Thus therefore, when I had heard and considered
what they said, I left them and went about my employ-
ment again, but their talk and discourse went with me ;
also my heart would tarry with them, for I was greatly
affected with their words, both because by them I was
convinced that I wanted the true tokens of a truly godly
man, and also because by them I was convinced of the
happy and blessed condition of him that was such a one.
Therefore I would often make it my business to be going
again and again into the company of these poor people,
for I could not stay away ; and the more I went among
them, the more I did question my condition ; and as I
still do remember, presently I found two things within
me at which I did sometimes marvel, especially considering what a blind, ignorant, sordid, and ungodly wretch
but just before I was. The one was a very great soft-
ness and tenderness of heart, which caused me to fall
under the conviction of what by Scripture they asserted ; and the other was a great bending in my mind to a
continual meditating on it and on all other good things
which at any time I heard or read of.

By these things my mind was now so turned that it
lay like a horse-leech at the vein, still crying out, Give,
give. My mind was so fixed on eternity and on the
things about the kingdom of heaven, that is, so far as I
knew, though as yet God knows I knew but little, that
neither pleasures, nor profits, nor persuasions, nor threats

could loose it or make it let go its hold; and though I may speak it with shame, yet it is in very deed a certain truth, it would then have been as difficult for me to have taken my mind from heaven to earth, as I have found it often since to get it again from earth to heaven.

One thing I may not omit. There was a young man in our town to whom my heart before was knit more than to any other; but he being a most wicked creature for cursing and swearing and uncleanness, I now shook him off and forsook his company. About a quarter of a year after I had left him, I met him in a certain lane and asked him how he did. He after his old swearing and mad way answered he was well. "But, Harry," said I, "why do you curse and swear thus? What will become of you if you die in this condition?" He answered me in a great chafe, "What would the devil do for company, if it were not for such as I am?"

About this time I met with some ranters' books that were put forth by some of our countrymen, which books were also highly in esteem by several old professors. Some of these I read, but was not able to make any judgment about them; wherefore as I read in them and thought upon them, seeing myself unable to judge, I would betake myself to hearty prayer in this manner:

"O Lord, I am a fool and not able to know the truth from error. Lord, leave me not to my own blindness, either to approve of or condemn this doctrine. If it be of God, let me not despise it; if it be of the devil, let me not embrace it. Lord, I lay my soul in this matter only at thy feet; let me not be deceived, I humbly beseech thee."

I had one religious companion all this while, and that was the poor man I spoke of before; but about this time he also turned a most devilish ranter, and gave himself up to all manner of filthiness, especially uncleanness.:

he would also deny that there was a God, angel, or spirit, and would laugh at all exhortations to sobriety. When I labored to rebuke his wickedness, he would laugh the more, and pretend that he had gone through all religions, and could never hit upon the right till now He told me also, that in a little time I should see all professors turn to the ways of the ranters. Wherefore, abominating those cursed principles, I left his company forthwith, and became to him as great a stranger as I had been before a familiar.

Neither was this man only a temptation to me, but my calling lying in the country, I happened to come into several people's company, who though strict in religion formerly, yet were also drawn away by these ranters. These would also talk with me of their ways, and condemn me as legal and dark, pretending that they only had attained to perfection, that they could do what they would and not sin. Oh, these temptations were suitable to my flesh, I being but a young man and my nature in its prime ; but God, who had as I hoped designed me for better things, kept me in the fear of his name, and did not suffer me to accept such cursed principles. And blessed be God, who put it into my heart to cry to him to be kept and directed, still distrusting mine own wisdom, for I have since seen even the effects of that prayer in his preserving me not only from ranting errors, but from those also that have sprung up since. The Bible was precious to me in those days.

And now methought I began to look into the Bible with new eyes, and read as I never did before ; and especially the epistles of the apostle Paul were sweet and pleasant to me ; and indeed, then I was never out of the Bible, either by reading or meditation, still crying out to God that I might know the truth and the way to heaven and glory. And as I went on and read, I hit upon that passage, "To one is given by the Spirit the word of wisdom ; to another, the word of knowledge by the same Spirit ; to another, faith," etc. 1 Cor. 12 : 8, 9. And though I have since seen that by this scripture the Holy Ghost intends in special things extraordinary, yet on me it did then fasten with conviction that I did want things ordinary, even that understanding and wisdom that other Christians had. On this word I mused, and could not tell what to do ; especially this word *faith* put me to it, for I could not help it, but sometimes must question whether I had any faith or no ; but I was loath to conclude I had no faith, for if I do so, thought I, then I shall count myself a very castaway indeed.

No, said I with myself, though I am convinced that I am an ignorant sot, and that I want those blessed gifts of knowledge and understanding that other people have, yet at a venture I will conclude I am not altogether faithless, though I know not what faith is ; for it was shown me, and that too, as I have seen since, by Satan, that those who conclude themselves in a faithless state have neither rest nor quiet in their souls, and I was loath to fall quite into despair.

Wherefore by this suggestion I was for a while made afraid to see my want of faith ; but God would not suffer me thus to undo and destroy my soul, but did continually against this my sad and blind conclusion create still within me such suppositions, insomuch that I could not rest content until I did now come to some certain knowledge whether I had faith or no, this always running in my mind : "But how if you want faith indeed ? But how can you tell you have faith ?" And besides, I saw for certain that if I had not, I was sure to perish for ever ; so that though I endeavored at the first to over-look the business of faith, yet in a little time, I better considering the matter, was willing to put myself upon the trial whether I had faith or no. But alas, poor wretch, so ignorant and brutish was I, that I knew not to this day any more how to do it, than I knew how to begin and accomplish a rare and curious piece of art which I never yet saw or considered.

Wherefore, while I was thus considering and being put to a plunge about it, for you must know that as yet I had not in this matter broken my mind to any one, only did hear and consider, the tempter came in with this delusion, that there was no way for me to know I had faith but by trying to work some miracles, urging those scriptures that seem to look that way for enforcing and strengthening his temptation. Nay, one day, as I was between Elstow and Bedford, the temptation was hot upon me to try if I had faith by doing some miracle, which miracle at this time was this : I must say to the puddles that were in the horse-pads, Be dry, and to the dry places, Be you puddles. And truly one time I was going to say so indeed ; but just as I was about to speak, this thought came into my mind, "But go under yonder hedge and pray first that God would make you able." But when I had concluded to pray, this came hot upon me, that if I prayed, and came again and tried to do it, and yet did nothing notwithstanding, then to be sure I had no faith, but was a castaway and lost ; nay, thought I, if it be so, I will not try yet, but will stay a little longer ; so I continued at a great loss, for I thought if they only had faith which could do such wonderful things, then I concluded that for the present I neither had it, nor yet for the time to come was ever like to have it. Thus I was tossed between the devil and my own ignorance, and so perplexed, especially at some times, that I could not tell what to do.

CHAPTER IV

About this time the state and happiness of these poor people at Bedford were thus in a kind of vision presented to me. I saw as if they were on the sunny side of some high mountain, there refreshing themselves with the pleasant beams of the sun, while I was shivering and shrinking in the cold, afflicted with frost, snow, and dark clouds. Methought also between me and them I saw a wall that did compass about this mountain. Now through this wall my soul did greatly desire to pass, concluding that if I could I would even go into the very midst of them, and there also comfort myself with the heat of their sun. About this wall I bethought myself to go again and again, still prying as I went to see if I could find some way or passage by which I might enter therein, but none could I find for some time. At the last I saw as it were a narrow gap, like a little doorway in the wall, through which I attempted to pass. Now the passage being very strait and narrow, I made many efforts to get in, but all in vain, even until I was well-nigh quite beat out by striving to get in; at last, with great striving, methought I at first did get in my head, and after that, by a sidelong striving, my shoulders and my whole body ; then I was exceeding glad, and went and sat down in the midst of them, and so was comforted with the light and heat of their sun.

Now this mountain and wall were thus made out to me. The mountain signified the church of the living God ; the sun that shone thereon, the comfortable shining of his merciful face on them that were therein : the wall I thought was the wall that did make separation between Christians and the world ; and the gap that was in the wall I thought was Jesus Christ, who is the way to God the Father. John 14 : 6 ; Matt. 7 : 14. But forasmuch as the passage was wonderful narrow, even so narrow that I could not but with great difficulty enter in thereat, it showed me that none could enter into life but those that were in downright earnest, and unless also they left that wicked world behind them, for here was only room for body and soul, but not for body and soul and sin. This resemblance abode upon my spirit many days, all which time I saw myself in a forlorn and sad condition, but yet was provoked to a vehement hunger and desire to be one of that number that did sit in the sunshine. Now also would I pray wherever I was, whether at home or abroad, in house or field ; and would also often, with lifting up of heart, sing that of the fifty-first Psalm, "O Lord, consider my distress," for as yet I knew not where it was.

Neither as yet could I attain to any comfortable persuasion that I had faith in Christ ; but instead of having satisfaction here, I began to find my soul to be assaulted with fresh doubts about my future happiness, especially with such as these : Whether I was elected. But how if the day of grace should be past and gone ? By these two temptations I was very much afflicted and disquieted, sometimes by one and sometimes by the other of them.

And first, to speak of that about my questioning my election, I found at this time that though I was in a flame to find the way to heaven and glory, and though nothing could beat me off from this, yet this question did so offend and discourage me that I was, especially sometimes, as if the very strength of my body also had been taken away by the force and power thereof. This scripture did also seem to me to trample upon all my desires : "It is not of him that willeth, nor of him that runneth,

but of God that showeth mercy." With this scripture I
could not tell what to do, for I evidently saw, unless the
great God of his infinite grace and bounty had volunta-
rily chosen me to be a vessel of mercy, though I should
desire and long and labor until my heart did break, no
good could come of it. Therefore this would stick with
me : How can you tell that you are elected ? And what
if you are not ? How then ? O Lord, thought I, what if
I am not indeed ? It may be you are not, said the tempter. It may be so indeed, thought I. Why then, said
Satan, you had as good leave off and strive no further ;
for if indeed you are not elected and chosen of God,
there is no hope of your being saved, for "it is not of
him that willeth, nor of him that runneth, but of God
that showeth mercy." Rom. 9 : 16. By these things I
was driven to my wits' end, not knowing what to say or
how to answer these temptations. Indeed, I little thought
that Satan had thus assaulted me, but thought it was
my own prudence thus to start the question : for that
the elect only obtained eternal life, that I without scru-
ple did heartily close withal ; but that myself was one
of them, there lay the question.

Thus therefore for several days I was greatly assaulted and perplexed, and was often, when I had been walking, ready to sink where I went with faintness in my
mind ; but one day, after I had been so many weeks
oppressed and cast down therewith, as I was now quite
giving up the ghost of all my hopes of ever attaining
life, that sentence fell with weight upon my spirit :
"Look at the generations of old, and see ; did ever any
trust in God, and were confounded ?" at which I was
greatly enlightened and encouraged in my soul, for thus
at that very instant it was expounded to me : "Begin at
the beginning of Genesis, and read to the end of the
Revelation, and see if you can find that there was ever

any that trusted in the Lord and was confounded." So coming home, I presently went to my Bible to see if I could find that saying, not doubting but to find it presently, for it was so fresh and with such strength and comfort on my spirit, that it was as if it talked with me. Well, I looked, but found it not, only it abode upon me. Then did I ask, first this good man and then another, if they knew where it was, but they knew no such place. At this I wondered that such a sentence should so suddenly and with such comfort and strength seize and abide upon my heart, and yet that none could find it, for I doubted not but that it was in the holy Scriptures. Thus I continued above a year, and could not find the place; but at last, casting my eye upon the Apocryphal books, I found it in Ecclesiasticus, 2 : 10. This at the first did somewhat daunt me; but because by this time I had got more experience of the love and kindness of God, it troubled me the less, especially when I considered that though it was not in those texts that we call holy and canonical, yet, forasmuch as this sentence was the sum and substance of many of the promises, it was my duty to take the comfort of it; and I bless God for that word, for it was of good to me : that word doth still ofttimes shine before my face.

After this that other doubt did come with strength upon me : But how if the day of grace should be past and gone? How if you have overstood the time of mercy? Now I remember that one day as I was walking in the country, I was much in the thoughts of this : But how if the day of grace is past? And to aggravate my trouble, the tempter presented to my mind those good people of Bedford, and suggested thus unto me : that these being converted already, they were all that God would save in those parts, and that I came too late, for these had got the blessing before I came. Now was

I in great distress, thinking in very deed that this might
well be so ; wherefore I went up and down bemoaning
my sad condition, counting myself far worse than a thousand fools for standing off thus long, and spending so
many years in sin as I had done, still crying out, Oh
that I had turned sooner ; Oh that I had turned seven
years ago. It made me also angry with myself to think
that I should have no more wit but to trifle away my
time till my soul and heaven were lost.

But when I had been long vexed with this fear, and
was scarce able to take one step more, just about the
same place where I received my other encouragement,
these words broke in upon my mind : "Compel them to
come in, that my house may be filled ; and yet there is
room." Luke 14 : 22. These words, but especially
those, "and yet there is room," were sweet words to me,
for truly I thought that by them I saw there was place
enough in heaven for me ; and moreover, that when the
Lord Jesus did speak these words, he then did think of
me, and that he, knowing that the time would come that
I should be afflicted with fear that there was no place
left for me in his bosom, did before speak this word, and
leave it upon record, that I might find help thereby
against this vile temptation. This I then verily believed. In the light and encouragement of this word I went
for some time ; and the comfort was the more when I
thought that the Lord Jesus should think on me so long
ago, and that he should speak those words on purpose
for my sake, for I did think verily that he did on purpose
speak them to encourage me withal.

But I was not without my temptations to go back
again—temptations, I say, both from Satan, mine own
heart, and carnal acquaintance ; but I thank God these
were outweighed by that sound sense of death and of
the day of judgment which abode as it were continually

in my view. I would often also think of Nebuchadnez-
zar, of whom it was said he had given him all the kingdoms of the earth. Dan. 5 : 18, 19. Yet, thought I, if
this great man had all his portion in this world, one hour
in hell-fire would make him forget all. This consideration was a great help to me.

I was almost made about this time to see something
concerning the beasts that Moses counted clean and unclean. I thought those beasts were types of men : the
clean, types of them that were the people of God ; but
the unclean, types of such as were children of the wicked one. Now I read that the clean beast chewed the
cud ; that is, thought I, they show us we must feed upon
the word of God. They also parted the hoof. I thought
that signified we must part, if we would be saved, with
the ways of ungodly men. And also, in further reading
about them, I found that though we did chew the cud as
the hare, yet if we walked with claws like a dog, or if
we did part the hoof like the swine, yet if we did not
chew the cud as the sheep, we are still for all that but
unclean ; for I thought the hare to be a type of those
that talk of the word, yet walk in the ways of sin, and
that the swine was like him that parteth with his outward pollution, but still wanteth the word of faith, without which there would be no way of salvation, let a man
be ever so devout. Deut. ch. 14. After this I found, by
reading the word, that those that must be glorified with
Christ in another world, must be called by him here—
called to the partaking of a share in his word and righteousness, and to the comforts and first-fruits of his Spirit, and to a peculiar interest in all those heavenly things
which do indeed prepare the soul for that rest and house
of glory which is in heaven above.

Here again I was at a very great stand, not knowing what to do, fearing I was not called ; for, thought I,

if I be not called, what then can do me good? None
but those who are effectually called, inherit the kingdom
of heaven. But Oh, how I now loved those words that
spoke of a Christian's calling; as when the Lord said to
one, "Follow me;" and to another, "Come after me;"
and Oh, thought I, that he would say so to me too; how
gladly would I run after him. I cannot now express
with what longings and breathings in my soul I cried to
Christ to call me. Thus I continued for a time all on a
flame to be converted to Jesus Christ; and did also see
at that day such glory in a converted state, that I could
not be contented without a share therein. Gold! could it
have been gotten for gold, what would I have given for
it! Had I had a whole world, it had all gone ten thousand times over for this, that my soul might have been
in a converted state. How lovely now was every one in
my eyes that I thought to be a converted man or woman. They shone; they walked like a people that carried
the broad seal of heaven about them. Oh, I saw the lot
was fallen to them in pleasant places, and that they had
a goodly heritage. Psalm 16 : 6.

But that which made me sick was that of Christ in
Mark, "He went up into a mountain, and called to him
whom he would, and they came unto him." Mark 3 : 13.
This scripture made me faint and fear, yet it kindled a
fire in my soul. That which made me fear was this, lest
Christ should have no liking to me, for he called whom
he would. But Oh, the glory that I saw in that condition
did still so engage my heart, that I could seldom read of
any that Christ did call, but I presently wished, Would
that I had been in their clothes ; would that I had been
born Peter'; would that I had been born John ; or would
that I had been by and heard him when he called them ;
how would I have cried, O Lord, call me also. But Oh,
I feared he would not call me.

And truly the Lord let me go thus many months together, and showed me nothing, either that I was already or should be called hereafter ; but at last, after much time spent and many groans to God that I might be made partaker of the holy and heavenly calling, that word came in upon me : "I will cleanse their blood that I have not cleansed ; for the Lord dwelleth in Zion." Joel 3 : 21. These words, I thought, were sent to encourage me to wait still upon God, and signified unto me, that if I were not already, yet the time might come when I might be in truth converted unto Christ.

About this time I began to break my mind to those poor people in Bedford, and to tell them my condition ; which when they had heard, they told Mr. Gifford of me, who himself also took occasion to talk with me, and was willing to be well persuaded of me, though, I think, from little grounds. But he invited me to his house, where I should hear him confer with others about the dealings of God with their souls ; from all which I still received more conviction, and from that time began to see something of the vanity and inward wretchedness of my wicked heart, for as yet I knew no great matter therein ; but now it began to be discovered unto me, and also to work at a rate it never did before.

Now I evidently found that lusts and corruptions put forth themselves within me in wicked thoughts and de-sires, which I did not regard before ; my desires also for heaven and life began to fail. I found also, that where-as before my soul was full of longing after God, now it began to hanker after every foolish vanity ; yea, my heart would not be moved to mind that which was good ; it began to be careless both of my soul and heaven. It would now continually hang back, both to and in every duty, and was as a clog upon the leg of a bird to hinder him from flying. Nay, thought I, now I grow worse and worse—now I am further from conversion than ever I was before; wherefore I began to sink greatly in my soul, and began to entertain such discouragement in my heart as laid me as low as hell. If now I should have burned at the stake I could not believe that Christ had a love for me; alas, I could neither hear him, nor see him, nor savor any of his things. I was driven as with a tempest; my heart would be unclean, and the Canaanites would dwell in the land.

Sometimes I would tell my condition to the people of God, which when they heard they would pity me, and would tell me of the promises; but they had as good have told me that I must reach the sun with my finger, as have bidden me receive or rely upon the promises, and as soon I should have done it. All my sense and feeling were against me, and I saw I had a heart that would sin, and that lay under a law that would condemn. These things have often made me think of the child which the father brought to Christ, who, while he was yet coming to him, was thrown down by the devil, and also so rent and torn by him that he lay and wallowed foaming. Mark 9 : 20; Luke 9 : 42.

Further, in these days I would find my heart to shut itself up against the Lord and against his holy word. I have found my unbelief to set as it were the shoulder to the door to keep him out, and that too even then when I have with many a bitter sigh cried, Good Lord, break it open; Lord, break these gates of brass, and cut these bars of iron asunder. Psa. 107 : 16. Yet that word would sometimes create in my heart a peaceful pause, "I girded thee, though thou hast not known me." Isa. 45 : 5. But all this while, as to the act of sinning, I was never more tender than now; my hinder parts were inward; I durst not take a pin or stick, though but so big as a straw, for my conscience now was sore, and would

smart at every touch. I could not now tell how to speak
my words, for fear I should misplace them. Oh, how
cautiously did I then go, in all I did or said. I found myself as in a miry bog, that shook if I did but stir, and
was as there left both of God and Christ and the Spirit,
and all good things.

But I observed, though I was such a great sinner
before conversion, yet God never much charged the guilt
of the sins of my ignorance upon me, only he showed me
I was lost if I had not Christ, because I had been a sinner. I saw that I wanted a perfect righteousness to
present me without fault before God, and this righteousness was nowhere to be found but in the person of
Jesus Christ. But my original and inward pollution,
that, that was my plague and affliction; that I saw at a
dreadful rate always putting forth itself within me; that
I had the guilt of to amazement; by reason of that, I
was more loathsome in mine own eyes than a toad, and
I thought I was so in God's eyes too. Sin and corruption, I said, would as naturally bubble out of my heart,
as water would bubble out of a fountain. I thought
now that every one had a better heart than I had. I
could have changed heart with any body. I thought
none but the devil himself could equal me for inward
wickedness and pollution of mind. I fell therefore, at
the sight of my own vileness, deeply into despair; for I
concluded that this condition that I was in could not
stand with a state of grace. Sure, thought I, I am
forsaken of God; sure I am given up to the devil, and
to a reprobate mind. And thus I continued for a long
while, even for some years together.

While I was thus afflicted with the fears of my own
damnation, there were two things would make me wonder. The one was, when I saw old people hunting after
the things of this life as if they should live here always.

the other was, when I found professors much distressed
and cast down when they met with outward losses, as
of husband, wife, child, etc. Lord, thought I, what ado
is here about such little things as these. What seeking
after carnal things by some, and what grief in others for
the loss of them. If they so much labor after and shed
so many tears for the things of this present life, how am
I to be bemoaned, pitied, and prayed for. My soul is
dying, my soul is damned. Were my soul but in a good
condition, and were I but sure of it, ah, how rich should
I esteem myself, though blessed but with bread and
water. I should count those but small afflictions, and
should bear them as little burdens. A wounded spirit
who can bear?

And though I was much troubled and tossed and
afflicted with the sight and sense and terror of my own
wickedness, yet I was afraid to let this sight and sense
go quite off my mind; for I found that unless guilt of
conscience was taken off the right way, that is, by the
blood of Christ, a man grew rather worse for the loss of
his trouble of mind than before. Wherefore, if my guilt
lay hard upon me, then would I cry that the blood of
Christ might take it off; and if it was going off without
it, for the sense of sin would be sometimes as if it would
die and go quite away, then I would also strive to fetch
it upon my heart again, by bringing the punishment of
sin in hell-fire upon my spirit, and would cry, Lord, let
it not go off my heart but in the right way, by the blood
of Christ and the application of thy mercy through him
to my soul, for that scripture did lay much upon me:
"Without the shedding of blood there is no remission."
Heb. 9:22. And that which made me the more afraid
of this was, because I had seen some, who though when
they were under the wounds of conscience would cry
and pray, yet feeling rather present ease for their trouble

than pardon for their sins, cared not how they lost their guilt, so they got it out of their minds. Now, having it got off the wrong way, it was not sanctified unto them; but they grew harder and blinder and more wicked after their trouble. This made me afraid, and made me cry to God the more that it might not be so with me. And now I was sorry that God had made me man, for I feared I was a reprobate. I counted man unconverted as the most doleful of all creatures. Thus being afflicted and tossed about my sad condition, I counted myself alone and above the most of men unblessed.

Yea, I thought it impossible that ever I should attain to so much godliness of heart as to thank God that he had made me a man. Man indeed is the most noble by creation of all creatures in the visible world; but by sin he has made himself the most ignoble. The beasts, birds, fishes, I have blessed their condition, for they had not a sinful nature; they were not obnoxious to the wrath of God; they were not to go to hell-fire after death. I could therefore have rejoiced had my condition been as any of theirs.

CHAPTER V

In this condition I went a great while; but when the comforting time was come, I heard one preach a sermon on these words in the Song, "Behold, thou art fair, my love; behold, thou art fair." Song 4 : 1. But at that time he made these two words, "my love," his chief subject-matter, from which, after he had a little opened the text, he drew these several conclusions : 1. That the church, and so every saved soul, is Christ's love when loveless; 2. Christ's love without a cause; 3. Christ's love which hath been hated of the world; 4. Christ's love when under temptation and under desertion; 5. Christ's love from first to last. But I got nothing by what he said at present, only when he came to the application of the fourth particular, this was the word he said : "If it be so that the saved soul is Christ's love when under temptation and desertion, then, poor tempted soul, when thou art assaulted and afflicted with temptations and the hidings of his face, yet think on these two words, 'my love,' still."

So as I was coming home, these words came again into my thoughts; and I well remember, as they came in, I said thus in my heart, What shall I get by thinking on these two words ? This thought had no sooner passed through my heart, but these words began thus to kindle in my spirit : "Thou art my love, thou art my love," twenty times together; and still as they ran in my mird they waxed stronger and warmer, and began to make me look up; but being as yet between hope and fear, I still replied in my heart, But is it true? but is it true? At which that sentence fell upon me, "He wist not that

it was true which was done unto him of the angel."
Acts 12 : 9.

Then I began to give place to the word, which with
power did over and over make this joyful sound within
my soul, "Thou art my love, thou art my love," and nothing shall separate thee from my love. And with that my
heart was filled full of comfort and hope, and now I
could believe that my sins would be forgiven me ; yea,
I was now so taken with the love and mercy of God, that
I remember I could not tell how to contain till I got
home. I thought I could have spoken of his love and
have told of his mercy to me, even to the very crows
that sat upon the ploughed lands before me, had they
been capable of understanding me ; wherefore I said in
my soul with much gladness, "Well, would I had a pen
and ink here, I would write this down before I go any
further ; for surely I shall not forget this, forty years
hence ;" but alas, within less than forty days I began to
question all again, which made me begin to question all
still.

Yet still at times I was helped to believe that it was
a true manifestation of grace unto my soul, though I
had lost much of the life and savor of it. Now about a
week or a fortnight after this I was much followed by
this scripture : " Simon, Simon, behold Satan hath desired
to have you." Luke 22 : 31. And sometimes it would
sound so loud within me, yea, and as it were call so
strongly after me, that once above all the rest I turned
my head over my shoulder, thinking verily that some
man had behind me called me. Being at a great dis-
tance, methought he called so loud, it came, as I have
thought since, to stir me up to prayer and to watchful-
ness. It came to acquaint me that a cloud and a storm
were coming down upon me ; but I understood it not.
Also, as I remember, that time that it called to me so

loud was the last time that it sounded in mine ears; but
methinks I hear still with what a loud voice these words,
"Simon, Simon," sounded in mine ears. I thought verily, as I have told you, that somebody had called after
me that was half a mile behind me; and although that
was not my name, yet it made me suddenly look behind
me, believing that he that called so loud meant me.

But so foolish was I and ignorant, that I knew not
the reason of this sound, which, as I did both see and
feel soon after, was sent from heaven as an alarm to
awaken me to provide for what was coming, only I
would muse and wonder in my mind to think what
should be the reason of this scripture, and that at this
rate so often and so loud it should still be sounding and
rattling in my ears; but, as I said before, I soon after
perceived the end of God therein; for about the space of
a month after, a very great storm came down upon me,
which handled me twenty times worse than all I had
met with before. It came stealing upon me, now by
one piece and then by another. First, all my comfort
was taken from me; then darkness seized upon me;
after which whole floods of blasphemies, both against
God, Christ, and the Scriptures, were poured upon my
spirit, to my great confusion and astonishment.

These blasphemous thoughts were such as stirred up
questions in me against the very being of God and of
his only beloved Son, as whether there were in truth a
God or Christ, and whether the holy Scriptures were not
rather a fable and cunning story, than the holy and pure
word of God. The tempter would also much assault me
with this: "How can you tell but that the Turks had as
good scriptures to prove their Mahomet the Saviour as
we have to prove our Jesus? and, could I think that so
many ten thousands in so many countries and kingdoms
should be without the knowledge of the right way to

heaven, if there were indeed a heaven, and that we only, who live in a corner of the earth, should alone be blessed therewith? Every one doth think his own religion right-est, Jews and Moors and Pagans; and how if all our faith and Christ and Scriptures should be but a think-so too?"

Sometimes I have endeavored to argue against these suggestions, and to set some of the sentences of blessed Paul against them; but alas, I quickly felt, when I thus did, such arguings as these would return again upon me: "Though we made so great a matter of Paul and of his words, yet how could I tell but that in very deed he, being a subtle and cunning man, might give himself up to deceive with strong delusions, and also take the pains and travail to undo and destroy his fellows?"

These suggestions, with many others which at this time I may not and dare not utter, neither by word nor pen, did make such a seizure upon my spirit, and did so overweigh my heart both with their number, continu-ance, and fiery force, that I felt as if there were nothing else but these from morning to night within me, and as though indeed there could be room for nothing else; and also concluded that God had in very wrath to my soul given me up to them, to be carried away with them as with a mighty whirlwind; only by the distaste that they gave unto my spirit, I felt there was something in me that refused to embrace them. But this consider-ation I then only had when God gave me leave to swal-low my spittle, otherwise the noise and strength and force of these temptations would drown and overflow, and as it were bury all such thoughts or the remem-brance of any such thing.

While I was in this temptation I often found my mind suddenly put upon it to curse and swear, or to speak some grievous thing against God, or Christ his

Son, or of the Scriptures. Now I thought, surely I am possessed of the devil. At other times, again, I thought I should be bereft of my senses ; for instead of lauding and magnifying God the Lord with others, if I but heard him spoken of, presently some most horrible blasphemous thought or other would bolt out of my heart against him ; so that whether I did think that God was, or again did think there was no such thing, no love, nor peace, nor gracious disposition could I feel within me.

These things did sink me into very deep despair, for I concluded that such things could not possibly be found among them that loved God. I often, when these temptations had been with force upon me, did compare myself to the case of a child whom some gipsy hath by force took up in her arms, and is carrying from friend and country. Kick sometimes I did, and also shriek and cry, but yet I was bound in the wings of the temptation, and the wind would carry me away. I thought also of Saul, and of the evil spirit that did possess him, and did greatly fear that my condition was the same with his. 1 Sam. 16 : 14.

In these days, when I have heard others talk of what was the sin against the Holy Ghost, then would the tempter so provoke me to desire to sin that sin, that I was as if I could not, must not, neither should be quiet until I had committed it. Now no sin would serve but that. If it were to be committed by the speaking of such a word, then I have been as if my mouth would have spoken that word, whether I would or no ; and in so strong a measure was this temptation upon me, that often I have been ready to clap my hands under my chin to hold my mouth from opening ; and to that end also I have had thoughts at other times to leap with my head downward into some muck-hole or other, to keep my mouth from speaking.

Now, again, I beheld the condition of the dog and toad, and counted the state of every thing that God had made far better than this dreadful state of mine and my companions. Yea, gladly would I have been in the condition of a dog or horse, for I knew they had no soul to perish under the everlasting weight of hell or sin, as mine was like to do. Nay, and though I saw this, felt this, and was. broken to pieces with it, yet that which added to my sorrow was, that I could not find that with all my soul I did desire deliverance. That scripture did also tear and rend my soul in the midst of these distractions: "The wicked are like the troubled sea, when it cannot rest, whose waters cast up mire and dirt. There is no peace, saith my God, to the wicked." Isa. 57 : 20, 21.

And now my heart was at times exceeding hard. If I would have given a thousand pounds for a tear, I could not shed one ; no, nor sometimes scarce desire to shed one. I was much dejected to think that this should be my lot. I saw some could mourn and lament their sin ; and others, again, could rejoice and bless God for Christ ; and others, again, could quietly talk of, and with gladness remember the word of God, while I only was in the storm or tempest. This much sunk me. I thought my condition was alone ; I would therefore much bewail my hard hap ; but get out of or get rid of these things I could not.

While this temptation lasted, which was about a year, I could attend upon none of the ordinances of God but with sore and great affliction ; yea, then I was most distressed with blasphemies. If I had been hearing the word, then uncleanness, blasphemies, and despair would hold me a captive there. If I had been reading, then sometimes I had sudden thoughts to question all I read ; sometimes, again, my mind would be so strangely snatched away and possessed with other things, that I have neither known, nor regarded, nor remembered so much as the sentence that but now I had read.

In prayer also I was greatly troubled at this time: sometimes I thought I felt Satan behind me pull my clothes ; he would be also continually at me in time of prayer, to have done : "Break off; make haste ; you have prayed enough, and stay no longer ;" still drawing my mind away. Sometimes also he would cast in such wicked thoughts as these : that I must pray to him, or for him. I have thought sometimes of that "fall down ;" or, "If thou wilt fall down and worship me." Matt. 4 : 9. Also when, because I have had wandering thoughts in the time of this duty, I have labored to compose my mind and fix it upon God, then with great force hath the tempter labored to distract me and confound me, and to turn away my mind by presenting to my heart and fancy the form of a bush, a bull, a besom, or the like, as if I should pray to these. To these he would also, at some times especially, so hold my mind, that I was as if I could think of nothing else, or pray to nothing else but to these, or such as they.

Yet at times I would have some strong and heart-affecting apprehensions of God and the reality of the truth of his gospel; but Oh, how would my heart at such times put forth itself with inexpressible groanings ! My whole soul was then in every word. I would cry with pangs after God, that he would be merciful unto me ; but then I would be daunted again with such conceits as these : I would think that God did mock at these my prayers, saying, and that in the audience of the holy angels, "This poor simple wretch doth hanker after me, as if I had nothing to do with my mercy but to bestow it on such as he. Alas, poor soul, how art thou deceived. It is not for such as thee to have favor with the Highest."

Then hath the tempter come upon me also with such discouragements as these : "You are very hot for mercy, but I will cool you ; this frame shall not last always. Many have been as hot as you for a time, but I have quenched their zeal ;" and with this, such and such who were fallen off would be set before mine eyes.   Then I would be afraid that I should do so too ; but, thought I, I am glad this comes into my mind. Well, I will watch, and take what care I can. "Though you do," said Satan, "I shall be too hard for you. I will cool you insensibly, by degrees, by little and little. What care I," saith he, "though I be seven years in chilling thy heart, if I can do it at last ? Continual rocking will lull a crying child asleep. I will ply it close, but I will have my end accomplished. Though you be burning hot at present, I can pull you from this fire. I shall have you cold before it be long."

These things brought me into great straits ; for as I at present could not find myself fit for present death, so I thought, to live long would make me yet more unfit, for time would make me forget all, and wear even the remembrance of the evil of sin, the worth of heaven, and the need I had of the blood of Christ to wash me, both out of mind and thought ; but I thank Christ Jesus, these things did not at present make me slack my crying, but rather did put me more upon it, like her who met with the adulterer, Deut. 22 : 27, in which days that was a good word to me, after I had suffered these things a while : "I am persuaded that neither death, nor life, nor angels, etc., shall separate us from the love of God, which is in Christ Jesus." Rom. 8 : 39. And now I hoped long life would not destroy me, nor make me miss of heaven.

I had some supports in this temptation, though they were then all questioned by me. That in Jer. 3 : 1, was

something to me; and so was the consideration of verse
four of that chapter, that though we have spoken and
done as evil things as we could, yet we shall cry unto
God, "My Father, thou art the guide of my youth," and
shall return unto him. I had also once a sweet glance
from that in 2 Cor. 5:21, "For he hath made him to be
sin for us, who knew no sin, that we might be made the
righteousness of God in him." I remember that one day,
as I was sitting in a neighbor's house, and there very
sad at the consideration of my many blasphemies, and
as I was saying in my mind, "What ground have I to
think that I, who have been so vile and abominable,
should ever inherit eternal life?" that word came suddenly upon me: "What shall we say to these things?
If God be for us, who can be against us?" That also
was a help unto me: "Because I live, you shall live
also." But these words were but hints, touches, and
short visits, though very sweet when present, only they
lasted not, but like Peter's sheet, of a sudden were
caught up from me to heaven again. Rom. 8:13; John
14:19; Acts 10:16.

But afterwards the Lord did more fully and graciously discover himself unto me, and indeed did quite not
only deliver me from the guilt that by these things was
laid upon my conscience, but also from the very filth
thereof; for the temptation was removed, and I was put
into my right mind again, as other Christians were. I
remember that one day, as I was travelling into the
country and musing on the wickedness and blasphemy
of my heart, and considering the enmity that was in me
to God, that scripture came into my mind: "Having
made peace through the blood of His cross." Col. 1:20.
By which I was made to see, both again and again, that
God and my soul were friends by his blood; yea, I saw
that the justice of God and my sinful soul could embrace

and kiss each other, through his blood. This was a good day to me ; I hope I shall never forget it.

At another time, as I sat by the fire in my house and was musing on my wretchedness, the Lord made that also a precious word unto me : "Forasmuch then as the children are partakers of flesh and blood, he also himself likewise took part of the same ; that through death he might destroy him that had the power of death, that is, the devil ; and deliver them who through fear of death were all their lifetime subject to bondage." Heb. 2 : 14, 15. I thought that the glory of these words was then so weighty on me, that I was both once and twice ready to swoon as I sat, yet not with grief and trouble, but with solid joy and peace.

CHAPTER VI

At this time also I sat under the ministry of holy Mr.
Gifford, whose doctrine, by God's grace, was much for
my stability. This man made it much his business to
deliver the people of God from all those hard and un-
sound tests that by nature we are prone to. He would
bid us take special heed that we took not up any truth
upon trust, as from this or that, or any other man or
men ; but cry mightily to God that he would convince
us of the reality thereof, and establish us therein by his
own Spirit in the holy word ; for, said he, if you do
otherwise, when temptation comes, if strongly upon you,
you not having received the word with evidence from
heaven, will find you want that help and strength now
to resist, that once you thought you had.

This was as seasonable to my soul as the former and
latter rain in their season, for I had found, and that by
sad experience, the truth of these his words ; for I had
felt that no man can say, especially when tempted by
the devil, that Jesus Christ is Lord, but by the Holy
Ghost. Wherefore I found my soul through grace very
apt to drink in this doctrine, and to incline to pray to
God that, in nothing that pertained to God's glory and
my own eternal happiness, he would suffer me to be
without the confirmation thereof from heaven ; for now I
saw clearly that there was an exceeding difference between the notion of the flesh and blood, and the revelation of God in heaven ; also a great difference between
that faith that is feigned and according to man's wisdom,
and that which comes by a man's being born thereto of
God.   Matt. 16 : 17 ; 1 John 5 : 1.

But Oh, how was my soul now led from truth to truth

by God; even from the birth and cradle of the Son of
God, to his ascension and second coming from heaven to
judge the world.   Truly I then found upon this account
the great God was very good unto me, for to my remembrance there was not any thing that I then cried unto
God to make known and reveal unto me, but he was
pleased to do it for me—I mean, not one part of the
gospel of the Lord Jesus, but I was orderly let into it.
Methought I saw, with great evidence from the four
evangelists, the wonderful works of God in giving Jesus
Christ to save us, from his conception and birth even to
his second coming to judgment: methought I was as if
I had seen him born, as if I had seen him grow up, as if
I had seen him walk through this world from the cradle
to the cross; to which also, when he came, I saw how
gently he gave himself to be crucified and nailed on the
cross for my sins and wicked doings.   Also, as I was
musing on this his progress, that passage dropped on
my spirit: He was ordained for the slaughter.   1 Pet.
1 : 11, 20.   When I have considered also the truth of his
resurrection, and have remembered that word, "Touch
me not, Mary," etc., I have seen as if he had leaped out
of the grave's mouth for joy that he was risen again,
and had got the conquest over our dreadful foes.   John
20 : 17.   I have also in the spirit seen him a man on the
right hand of God the Father for me; and have seen the
manner of his coming from heaven to judge the world
with glory, and have been confirmed in these things by
these scriptures: Acts 1 : 9; 7 : 56; 10 : 42; Heb. 7 : 24;
Rev. 1 : 18; 1 Thess. 4 : 17, 18.

Once I was troubled to know whether the Lord Jesus
was man as well as God, and God as well as man; and
truly in those days, let men say what they would, unless
I had it with evidence from heaven, all was nothing to
me; I counted myself not set down in any truth of God.

Well, I was much troubled about this point, and could not tell how to be resolved; at last that in Rev. 5 : 6 came into my mind : "And I beheld, and lo, in the midst of the throne and of the four beasts, and in the midst of the elders, stood a Lamb." In the midst of the throne, thought I, there is the Godhead; in the midst of the elders, there is manhood. Oh, methought this did glister. It was a goodly touch, and gave me sweet satisfaction. That other scripture also did help me much in this : "Unto us a child is born, unto us a son is given : and the government shall be upon his shoulder : and his name shall be called Wonderful, Counsellor, The mighty God, The everlasting Father, The Prince of Peace." Isa. 9 : 6. Also, besides these teachings of God in his word, the Lord made use of two things to confirm me in this truth : the one was the errors of the fanatics, and the other was the guilt of sin; for as the fanatics did oppose the truth, so God did the more confirm me in it by leading me into the scripture that did wonderfully maintain it.

The errors they maintained were,

1. That the holy Scriptures were not the word of God.

2. That every man in the world had the Spirit of Christ, grace, faith, etc.

3. That Christ Jesus, as crucified and dying sixteen hundred years ago, did not satisfy divine justice for the sins of the people.

4. That Christ's flesh and blood were within the saints.

5. That the bodies of the good and bad that are buried in the churchyard shall not rise again.

6. That the resurrection is passed with good men already.

7. That that man Jesus that was crucified between

two thieves on mount Calvary, in the land of Canaan, by Judea, was not ascended above the starry heaven.

8. That he should not, even the same Jesus that died by the hands of the Jews, come again at the last day, and as man judge all nations, etc.

Many more vile and abominable things were in those days fomented by them, by which I was driven to a more narrow search of the Scriptures, and was, through their light and testimony, not only enlightened, but greatly confirmed and comforted in the truth.

And as I said, the guilt of sin did help me much, for still, as that would come upon me, the blood of Christ did take it off again and again, and that too sweetly, according to the Scriptures. Oh, friends, cry to God to reveal Jesus Christ unto you; there is none teacheth like him.

It would be too long here to stay to tell you in particular how God did confirm me in all the things of Christ; and how he did, that he might do so, lead me into his words; yea, and also how he did open them unto me, and make them shine before me, and cause them to dwell with me, talk with me, and comfort me over and over, both of his own being and the being of his Son and Spirit, and word and gospel. Only this, as I said before, I will say unto you again, that in general he was pleased to take this course with me: first to suffer me to be afflicted with temptations concerning them, and then reveal them unto me. As sometimes I would lie under great guilt for sin, even crushed to the ground therewith, and then the Lord would show me the death of Christ; yea, so sprinkle my conscience with his blood, that I would find, and that before I was aware, that in that conscience, where but just now did reign and rage the law, even there would rest and abide the peace and love of God, through Christ.

Now I had an evidence, as I thought, of my salva-

tion from heaven, with many golden seals thereon, all
hanging in my sight; now could I remember this manifestation, and the other discovery of grace with comfort;
and would often long and desire that the last day were
come, that I might be for ever inflamed with the sight
and joy and communion with Him whose head was crown-
ed with thorns, whose face was spit upon, and body broken, and soul made an offering for my sins ; for whereas
before I lay continually trembling at the mouth of hell,
now methought I was got so far therefrom that when I
looked back I could scarce discern it; and Oh, thought
I, that I were fourscore years old now, that I might die
quickly, that my soul might be gone to rest.

But before I had got thus far out of these my temptations, I did greatly long to see some ancient godly
man's experience, who had written some hundreds of
years before I was born ; for those who had written in
our days, I thought—but I desire them now to pardon
me—that they had written only that which others felt ;
or else had, through the strength of their wits and parts,
studied to answer such objections as they perceived
others were perplexed with, without going down themselves into the deep.

Well, after many such longings in my mind, the God
in whose hands are all our days and ways, did cast into
my hand one day a book of Martin Luther's ; it was his
Comment on the Galatians. It also was so old that it
was ready to fall piece from piece, if I did but turn it
over. Now I was pleased much that such an old book
had fallen into my hands, the which when I had but a
little way perused I found my condition in his experience
so largely and profoundly handled, as if his book had
been written out of my heart. This made me marvel,
for thus thought I : this man could not know any thing
of the state of Christians now, but must needs write and

speak the experience of former days. Besides, he doth
most gravely also in that book debate of the rise of these
temptations, namely, blasphemy, desperation, and the
like; showing that the law of Moses, as well as the
devil, death, and hell, hath a very great hand therein, the
which at first was very strange to me; but considering
and watching, I found it so indeed. But of particulars
here I intend nothing, only this methinks I must let fall
before all men: I do prefer this book of Martin Luther
upon the Galatians, excepting the Holy Bible, before all
the books that ever I have seen, as most fit for a wounded conscience.

And now I found, as I thought, that I loved Christ
dearly. Oh, methought my soul cleaved unto him, my
affections cleaved unto him; I felt my love to him as hot
as fire; and now, as Job said, I thought I should die in
my nest: but I quickly found that my great love was
but too little, and that I, who had, as I thought, such
burning love to Jesus Christ, could let him go again for
a very trifle. God can tell how to abase us, and can
hide pride from man.

Quickly after this my love was tried to purpose; for
after the Lord had in this manner thus graciously delivered me from this great and sore temptation, and had
established me so sweetly in the faith of his holy gospel,
and had given me such strong consolation and blessed
evidence from heaven touching my interest in his love
through Christ, the tempter came upon me again, and
that with a more grievous and dreadful temptation than
before: and that was, to sell and part with this most
blessed Christ—to exchange him for the things of this
life, for any thing. The temptation lay upon me for the
space of a year, and did follow me so continually that I
was not rid of it one day in a month; no, not sometimes
one hour in many days together, unless when I was

asleep. And though in my judgment I was persuaded that those who were once effectually in Christ, as I hoped through his grace I had seen myself, could never lose him for ever : for " the land shall not be sold for ever ; for the land is mine," saith God. Lev. 25 : 23. Yet it was a continual vexation to me to think that I should have so much as one such thought within me against a Christ, a Jesus who had done for me as he had done ; and yet then I had almost none others but such blasphemous ones.

It was neither my dislike of the thought, nor yet any desire and endeavor to resist it, that in the least did shake or abate the continuation or force and strength thereof ; for it did always, in almost whatever I thought, intermix itself therewith in such sort that I could neither eat my food, stoop for a pin, chop a stick, or cast mine eyes to look on this or that, but still the temptation would come, Sell Christ for this, or sell Christ for that ; sell him, sell him. Sometimes it would run in my thoughts not so little as a hundred times together, Sell him, sell him, sell him ; against which I may say, for whole hours together I have been forced to stand as continually leaning and forcing my spirit against it, lest haply before I was aware some wicked thought might arise in my heart that might consent thereto ; and sometimes the tempter would make me believe I had consented to it ; but then I would be as tortured upon a rack for whole days together.

This temptation did put me to such fears lest I should at sometimes, I say, consent thereto and be overcome therewith, that by the very force of my mind in laboring to gainsay and resist this wickedness, my very body would be put in action or motion, by way of pushing or thrusting with my hands or elbows, still answering as fast as the destroyer said, "Sell him," "I will not, I will not, I will not ; no, not for thousands. thousands, thousands of worlds;" thus reckoning, lest I should in the midst of these assaults set too low a value on him, even until I scarce well knew where I was, or how to be composed again. At these seasons he would not let me eat my food in quiet; but forsooth, when I was set at the table at my meat, I must go hence to pray; I must leave my food now, and just now, so counterfeit holy would this devil be. When I was thus tempted, I would say in myself, Now I am at meat, let me make an end. No, said he, you must do it now, or you will displease God and despise Christ. Wherefore I was much afflicted with these things, and because of the sinfulness of my nature. If, imagining that these were impulses from God, I should deny to do it, would it not be as if I denied God? and then should I not be as guilty, because I did obey a temptation of the devil, as if I had broken the law of God indeed?

But to be brief, one morning as I lay in my bed I was, as at other times, most fiercely assaulted with this temptation to sell and part with Christ, the wicked suggestion still running in my mind, "Sell him, sell him, sell him, sell him," as fast as a man could speak; against which also in my mind, as at other times, I answered, "No, no, not for thousands, thousands, thousands," at least twenty times together; but at last, after much striving, even until I was almost out of breath, I felt this thought pass through my heart, "Let him go if he will;" and I thought also that I felt my heart freely consent thereto. Oh the diligence of Satan; Oh the desperateness of man's heart!

Now was the battle won, and down fell I, as a bird that is shot from the top of a tree, into great guilt and fearful despair. Thus getting out of my bed, I went moping into the fields; but, God knows, with as heavy a heart as mortal man I think could bear, where for the

space of two hours I was like a man bereft of life, and
as now past all recovery, and bound over to eternal punishment.

And withal that scripture did seize upon my soul:
"Or profane person, as Esau, who for one morsel of meat
sold his birthright. For ye know how that afterwards,
when he would have inherited the blessing, he was
rejected; for he found no place of repentance, though he
sought it carefully with tears." Heb. 12:16, 17.

Now was I as one bound; I felt myself shut up into
the judgment to come. Nothing now, for two years
together, would abide with me but damnation, and an
expectation of damnation; I say, nothing now would
abide with me but this, save some few moments for
relief, as in the sequel you will see. These words were
to my soul like fetters of brass to my legs, in the continual sound of which I went for several months together.
But about ten or eleven o'clock on that day, as I was
walking under a hedge, full of sorrow and guilt, God
knows, and bemoaning myself for this hard hap that
such a thought should arise within me, suddenly this
sentence rushed in upon me: "The blood of Christ remits
all guilt." At this I made a stand in my spirit. With
that this word took hold upon me: "The blood of Jesus
Christ his Son cleanseth us from all sin." 1 John 1:7.

Now I began to conceive peace in my soul; and methought I saw as if the tempter did leer and steal away
from me, as being ashamed of what he had done. At the
same time also I had my sin and the blood of Christ thus
represented to me: that my sin, when compared to the
blood of Christ, was no more to it than this little clod or
stone before me is to this vast and wide field that here I
see. This gave me good encouragement for the space of
two or three hours; in which time also methought I saw
by faith the Son of God as suffering for my sins: but

because it tarried not, I therefore sunk in my spirit under exceeding guilt again; but chiefly by the afore-mentioned scripture concerning Esau's selling of his birthright, for that scripture would lie all day long in my mind, and hold me down, so that I could by no means lift up myself; for when I would strive to turn to this scripture or that for relief, still that sentence would be sounding in me: "For ye know how that afterwards, when he would have inherited the blessing, he found no place of repentance, though he sought it carefully with tears." Sometimes, indeed, I would have a touch from that in Luke 22 : 32 : "I have prayed for thee, that thy faith fail not;" but it would not abide upon me; neither could I indeed, when I considered my state, find ground to conceive in the least that there should be the root of that grace in me, having sinned as I had done. Now was I torn and rent in a heavy case for many days together.

Then began I with sad and careful heart to consider of the nature and largeness of my sin, and to search into the word of God, if I could in any place espy a word of promise, or any encouraging sentence, by which I might take relief. Wherefore I began to consider that of Mark 3 : 28 : "All sins shall be forgiven unto the sons of men, and blasphemies wherewith soever they shall blaspheme." Which place, methought at a blush, did contain a large and glorious promise for the pardon of high offences; but considering the place more fully, I thought it was rather to be understood as relating more chiefly to those who had, while in a natural state, com-mitted such things as there are mentioned; but not to me, who had not only received light and mercy, but who had, both after and also contrary to that, so slighted Christ as I had done. I feared therefore that this wick-ed sin of mine might be that sin unpardonable of which he there thus speaketh: "But he that shall blaspheme

against the Holy Ghost hath never forgiveness, but is in
danger of eternal damnation." Mark 3 : 29 And I did
the rather give credit to this, because of that sentence
in the Hebrews: "For ye know how that afterwards,
when he would have inherited the blessing, he was
rejected; for he found no place of repentance, though he
sought it carefully with tears." And this stuck always
with me. And now was I both a burden and a terror to
myself; nor did I ever so know as now what it was to
be weary of my life, and yet afraid to die. Oh, how
gladly now would I have been any body but myself—
any thing but a man, and in any condition but my own;
for there was nothing did pass more frequently over my
mind than that it was impossible for me to be forgiven
my transgression, and be saved from the wrath to come.

And now I began to labor to call again time that was
past, wishing a thousand times twice told that the day
was yet to come when I should be tempted to such a
sin; concluding with great indignation, both against
my heart and all assaults, how I would rather be torn in
piêces than be found a consenter thereto. But alas,
these thoughts and wishes and resolvings were now too
late to help me; this thought had passed my heart:
God hath let me go, and I am fallen. Oh, thought I,
that it was with me as in months past, as in the days
when God preserved me. Job 29 : 2.

Then again, being loath and unwilling to perish, I
began to compare my sin with others, to see if I could
find that any of those that were saved had done as I had
done. So I considered David's adultery and murder, and
found them most heinous crimes, and those too committed after light and grace received. But yet, by considering that his transgressions were only such as were
against the law of Moses, from which the Lord Christ
could, with the consent of his word, deliver him; but

mine was against the gospel, yea, against the Mediator thereof; I had sold my Saviour: now again would I be as if racked upon the wheel, when I considered that besides the guilt that possessed me, I should be so void of grace, so bewitched. What, thought I, must it be no sin but this? Must it needs be the great transgression? Must that wicked one touch my soul? Psa. 19:13; 1 John 5:18. Oh, what sting did I find in all these sentences! What, thought I, is there but one sin that is unpardonable—but one sin that layeth the soul without the reach of God's mercy? and must I be guilty of that; must it needs be that? Is there but one sin, among so many millions of sins, for which there is no forgiveness; and must I commit this? Oh unhappy sin! Oh unhappy man! These things would so break and confound my spirit, that I could not tell what to do; I thought at times they would have broken my wits: and still to aggravate my misery, that would run in my mind: "Ye know how that afterwards, when he would have inherited the blessing, he was rejected." Oh, no one knows the terrors of those days but myself.

CHAPTER VII

AFTER this I began to consider of Peter's sin, which he committed in denying his Master. And indeed this came nighest to mine of any that I could find, for he had denied his Saviour as I, after light and mercy received; yea, and that too after warning given him. I also considered that he did it once and twice, and that after time to consider between. But though I put all these circumstances together, that, if possible, I might find help, yet I considered again that his was but a denial of his Master, but mine was a selling of my Saviour. Wherefore I thought with myself that I came nearer to Judas than either to David or Peter. Here, again, my torment would flame out and afflict me; yea, it would grind me as it were to powder, to consider the preservation of God towards others while I fell into the snare; for in my thus considering other men's sins, and comparing them with mine own, I could evidently see that God preserved them, notwithstanding their wickedness, and would not let them, as he had let me, become a son of perdition.

But Oh, how did my soul at this time prize the preservation that God did set about his people. Ah, how safely did I see them walk whom God had hedged in. They were within his care, protection, and special providence; though they were full as bad as I by nature, yet because he loved them, he would not suffer them to fall without the range of mercy; but as for me, I was gone; I had done it; he would not preserve me, nor keep me; but suffered me, because I was a reprobate, to fall as I had done. Now did those blessed places that speak of God's keeping his people shine like the sun before me, though not to comfort me, yet to show me the blessed state and heritage of those whom the Lord had blessed.

Now I saw that as God had his hand in all the providences and dispensations that overtook his elect, so he had his hand in all the temptations that they had to sin against him, not to animate them to wickedness, but to choose their temptations and troubles for them, and also to leave them for a time to such things only as might not destroy, but humble them—as might not put them beyond, but lay them in the way of the renewing of his mercy. But Oh, what love, what care, what kindness and mercy did I now see mixing itself with the most severe and dreadful of all God's ways to his people. He would let David, Hezekiah, Solomon, Peter, and others fall, but he would not let them fall into the sin unpardonable, nor into hell for sin. Oh, thought I, these be the men that God hath loved; these be the men that God, though he chastiseth them, keeps in safety by him, and whom he makes to abide under the shadow of the Almighty.

But all these thoughts added sorrow, grief, and horror to me, as whatever I now thought on it was killing to me. If I thought how God kept his own, that was killing to me; if I thought of how I was fallen myself, that was killing to me. As all things wrought together for the best, and to do good to them that were the called according to his purpose; so I thought that all things wrought for damage and for my eternal overthrow. Then, again, I began to compare my sin with the sin of Judas, that if possible I might find if mine differed from that which in truth is unpardonable; and Oh, thought I, if it should differ from it, though but the breadth of a hair, what a happy condition is my soul in. And by considering I found that Judas did his intentionally, but

mine was against prayer and strivings ; besides, his was
committed with such deliberation, but mine in a fearful
hurry on a sudden : all this while I was tossed to and fro
like the locust, and driven from trouble to sorrow, hearing always the sound of Esau's fall in mine ears, and
the dreadful consequences thereof.

This consideration about Judas' sin was for a while
some little relief to me, for I saw I had not, as to the
circumstances, transgressed so fully as he.   But this
was quickly gone again, for I thought with myself there
might be more ways than one to commit this unpardonable sin ; also I thought there might be degrees of that
as well as of other transgressions ; wherefore, for aught
I yet could perceive, this iniquity of mine might be such
as might never be passed by.   I was often now ashamed
that I should be like such an ugly man as Judas.   I
thought also how loathsome I should be unto all the
saints in the day of judgment, insomuch that now I
could scarce see a good man that I believed had a good
conscience, but I would feel my heart tremble at him
while I was in his presence.   Oh, now I saw a glory in
walking with God, and what a mercy it was to have a
good conscience before him.

I was much about this time tempted to content myself by receiving some false opinions, as that there
should be no such thing as a day of judgment ; that we
should not rise again ; and that sin was no such grievous thing; the tempter suggesting thus : "If these
things should indeed be true, yet to believe otherwise
would yield you ease for the present.   If you must perish, never torment yourself so much beforehand ; drive
the thoughts of damning out of your mind by possessing
your mind with some such conclusions that atheists and
ranters use to help themselves withal."   But Oh, when
such thoughts have fled through my heart, how, as it

were within a step, have death and judgment been in my view! Methought the Judge stood at the door; I was as if it was come already, so that such things could have no entertainment. But methinks I see by this that Satan will use any means to keep the soul from Christ; he loveth not an awakened frame of spirit; security, blindness, darkness, and error are the very kingdom and habitation of the wicked one. I found it a hard work now to pray to God, because despair was swallowing me up; I thought I was as with a tempest driven away from God, for always when I cried to God for mercy this would come in: "It is too late; I am lost; God hath let me fall, not to my correction but my condemnation; my sin is unpardonable, and I know concerning Esau, how that, after he had sold his birthright, he would have received the blessing, but was rejected."

About this time I did light on that dreadful story of that miserable mortal, Francis Spira, a book that was to my troubled spirit as salt when rubbed into a fresh wound. Every sentence in that book, every groan of that man, with all the rest of his actions in his dolors, as his tears, his prayers, his gnashing of teeth, his wringing of hands, his twisting and languishing and pining away under that mighty hand of God that was upon him, were as knives and daggers in my soul; especially that sentence of his was frightful to me: "Man knows the beginning of sin, but who bounds the issues thereof?" Then would the former sentence, as the conclusion of all, fall like a hot thunderbolt again upon my conscience: "For ye know how that afterwards, when he would have inherited the blessing, he was rejected; for he found no place of repentance, though he sought it carefully with tears."

Then would I be struck into a very great trembling, insomuch that at some times I could, for whole days

together, feel my very body as well as my mind shake
and totter under the sense of this dreadful judgment of
God that would fall on those that have sinned that most
fearful and unpardonable sin.   I felt also such a clog-
ging and heat at my stomach, by reason of this my terror, that I was, especially at some times, as if my breast-
bone would split asunder ; then I thought concerning
that of Judas, who by his falling headlong burst asunder,
and all his bowels gushed out.   Acts 1 : 18.   I feared
also that this was the mark that God did set on Cain,
even continual fear and trembling, under the heavy load
of guilt that he had charged on him for the blood of his
brother Abel.

Thus did I wind and twine and shrink under the burden that was upon me, which burden did so oppress me
that I could neither stand nor go, nor lie either at rest or
quiet.   Yet that saying would sometimes come into my
mind : " He hath received gifts for the rebellious."   Psa.
68 : 18.   The rebellious, thought I : why, surely they are
such as once were under subjection to their prince ; even
those who, after they have once sworn subjection to his
government, have taken up arms against him ; and this,
thought I, is my very condition.   I once loved him, feared
him, served him ; but now I am a rebel ; I have sold him ;
I have said, Let him go if he will : but yet he has gifts
for rebels ; and then why not for me ?   This sometimes
I thought on, and would labor hard to take hold thereof,
that some, though small refreshment, might have been
conceived by me ; but in this also I missed of my desire :
I was driven with force beyond it ; I was like a man
going to execution even by that place where he would
fain creep in and hide himself, but may not.

Again, after I had thus considered the sins of the
saints in particular, and found mine went beyond them,
then I began to think with myself, Set the case as I

should, put all theirs together, and mine alone against them, might I not then find encouragement ? for if mine, though bigger than any one, yet should be but equal to all, then there is hope ; for that blood that hath virtue enough in it to wash away all theirs, hath virtue enough in it to wash away mine, though this one be full as big, if not bigger than all theirs. Here, again, I would consider the sin of David, of Solomon, of Manasseh, of Peter, and the rest of the great offenders, and would also labor, what I might with fairness, to aggravate and heighten their sins by several circumstances. I would think with myself that David shed blood to cover his adultery, and that by the sword of the children of Ammon—a work that could not be done but by contrivance, which was a great aggravation to his sin.

But then this would turn upon me : "Ah, but these were but sins against the law, from which there was a Jesus sent to save them ; but yours is a sin against the Saviour, and who shall save you from that ?" Then I thought on Solomon, and how he sinned in loving strange women, in falling away to their idols, in building them temples, in doing this after light, in his old age, after great mercy received. But the same conclusion that cut me off in the former consideration, cut me off as to this, namely, that all these were but sins against the law, for which God had provided a remedy ; but I had sold my Saviour, and there remained no more sacrifice for sin. I would then add to these men's sins the sins of Manasseh, how that he built altars for idols in the house of the Lord ; he also observed times, used enchantments, had to do with wizards, was a wizard, had his familiar spirits, burned his children in sacrifice to devils, and made the streets of Jerusalem run down with the blood of innocents   These, thought I, are great sins, sins of a bloody color ; but yet it would turn again upon me :

"They are none of them of the nature of yours; you have parted with Jesus, you have sold your Saviour." This one consideration would always kill my heart : my sin was point-blank against my Saviour, and that too at such a height that I had in my heart said of him, Let him go if he will. Oh, methought this sin was bigger than the sins of a country, of a kingdom, or of the whole world; no one pardonable, nor all of them together was able to equal mine; mine outwent them every one.

Now I would find my mind to flee from God as from the face of a dreadful judge; yet this was my torment, I could not escape his hand : "It is a fearful thing to fall into the hands of the living God." Heb. 10 : 31. But blessed be his grace, that scripture in these flying fits would call, as running after me : "I have blotted out, as a thick cloud, thy transgressions, and as a cloud, thy sins : return unto me; for I have redeemed thee." Isa. 44 : 22. This, I say, would come in upon my mind when I was fleeing from the face of God, for I did flee from his face, that is, my mind and spirit fled before him, by reason of his highness I could not endure; then would the text cry, "Return unto me;" it would cry aloud with a very great voice, "Return unto me; for I have redeemed thee."

Indeed, this would make me make a little stop, and as it were look over my shoulder behind me to see if I could discern that the God of grace did follow me with a pardon in his hand; but I could no sooner do that but all would be clouded and darkened again by that sentence : "For ye know how that afterwards, when he would have inherited the blessing, he found no place of repentance, though he sought it carefully with tears." Wherefore I could not refrain, but fled, though at sometimes it cried, Return, return, as if it did follow after me; but I feared to close in therewith lest it should not come from God, for that other, as I said, was still sounding in my conscience: "For ye know how that afterwards, when he would have inherited the blessing, he was rejected," etc.

Once, as I was walking to and fro in a good man's shop, bemoaning myself in my sad and doleful state, afflicting myself with self-abhorrence for this wicked and ungodly thought; lamenting also this hard hap of mine, that I should commit so great a sin, greatly fearing that I should not be pardoned; praying also in my heart that if this sin of mine did differ from that against the Holy Ghost, the Lord would show it me; and being now ready to sink with fear, suddenly there was as if there had rushed in at the window the noise of wind upon me, but very pleasant, and as if I heard a voice speaking, "Didst thou ever refuse to be justified by the blood of Christ?" and withal, my whole life of profession past was in a moment opened unto me, wherein I was made to see that designedly I had not; so my heart answered groaningly, No.

Then fell with power that word of God upon me: "See that ye refuse not him that speaketh." Heb. 12: 25. This made a strange seizure upon my spirit; it brought light with it, and commanded a silence in my heart of all those tumultuous thoughts that did before use, like masterless hell-hounds, to roar and bellow and make a hideous noise within me. It showed me also that Jesus Christ had yet a word of grace and mercy for me; that he had not, as I had feared, quite forsaken and cast off my soul; yea, this was a kind of check for my proneness to desperation—a kind of threatening of me, if I did not, notwithstanding my sins and the heinousness of them, venture my salvation upon the Son of God.

But as to my determining about this strange dispen-

sation, what it was I know not, or from whence it came
I know not; I have not yet in twenty years' time been
able to make a judgment of it; I thought then what I
should be loath here to speak. But verily that sudden
rushing wind was as if an angel had come upon me;
but both it and the salvation I will leave until the day
of judgment: only this I say, it commanded a great
calm in my soul; it persuaded me there might be hope;
it showed me, as I thought, what the sin unpardonable
was, and that my soul had yet the blessed privilege to
flee to Jesus Christ for mercy. But I say, concerning
this dispensation, I know not yet what to say of it;
which was also in truth the cause that at first I did not
speak of it in the book; I do now also leave it to be
thought on by men of sound judgment. I lay not the
stress of my salvation thereupon, but upon the Lord
Jesus in the promise; yet seeing I am here unfolding
my secret things, I thought it might not be altogether
inexpedient to let this also show itself, though I cannot
now relate the matter as then I did experience it. This
lasted in the savor of it for about three or four days, and
then I began to mistrust and to despair again.

Wherefore still my life hung in doubt before me, not
knowing which way I should go; only this I found my
soul desire, even to cast itself at the foot of grace by
prayer and supplication. But Oh, it was hard for me
now to have the face to pray to this Christ for mercy
against whom I had thus vilely sinned; it was hard
work, I say, to offer to look Him in the face against whom
I had so vilely sinned; and indeed I have found it as
difficult to come to God by prayer, after backsliding from
him, as to do any other thing. Oh the shame that did
now attend me, especially when I thought, I am now
a going to pray to him for mercy that I had so lightly
esteemed but a while before; I was ashamed, yea, even

confounded, because this villany had been committed by
me ; but I saw that there was but one way with me : I
must go to him, and humble myself unto him, and beg
that he of his wonderful mercy would show pity to me,
and have mercy upon my wretched sinful soul ; which,
when the tempter perceived, he strongly suggested to me
that "I ought not to pray to God, for prayer was not for
any in my case ; neither could it do me good, because I
had rejected the Mediator, by whom all prayers came
with acceptance to God the Father, and without whom no
prayer could come into his presence ; wherefore now to
pray is but to add sin to sin ; yea, now to pray, seeing
God hath cast you off, is the next way to anger and
offend him more than you ever did before. For God,
saith he, hath been weary of you for these several years
already, because you are none of his ; your bawling in
his ears hath been no pleasant voice to him, and therefore he let you sin this sin, that you might be quite cut
off : and will you pray still ?"

This the devil urged, and set forth that in Numbers,
when Moses said to the children of Israel, that because
they would not go up to possess the land when God
would have them, therefore for ever he did bar them out
from thence, though they prayed they might with tears.
Num. 14 : 36, etc. As it is said in another place, "The
man that sins presumptuously shall be taken from God's
altar, that he may die ;" even as Joab was by king Solomon, when he thought to find shelter there. Exodus
21 : 14 ; 1 Kings 2 : 28–34. These places did pinch me
very sore ; yet, my case being desperate, I thought with
myself, I can but die ; and if it must be so, it shall once
be said that such an one died at the foot of Christ in
prayer. This I did, but with great difficulty, God doth
know ; and that because, together with this, still that
saying about Esau would be set at my heart, even like

a flaming sword, to keep the way of the tree of life, lest I should take thereof and live.

Oh, who knows how hard a thing I found it to come to God in prayer. I did also desire the prayers of the people of God for me; but I feared that God would give them no heart to do it; yea, I trembled in my soul to think that some or other of them would shortly tell me that God had said those words to them that he once did say to the prophet concerning the children of Israel: "Pray not for this people, for I will not hear them," Jer. 11 : 14; so pray not for him, for I have rejected him. Yea, I thought that he had whispered this to some of them already, only they durst not tell me so; neither durst I ask them of it, for fear, if it should be so, it would make me quite beside myself. "Man knows the beginning of sin," said Spira, "but who bounds the issues thereof?"

About this time I took an opportunity to break my mind to an ancient Christian, and told him all my case; I told him also that I was afraid that I had sinned the sin against the Holy Ghost; and he told me he thought so too. Here therefore I had but cold comfort; but talking a little more with him, I found him, though a good man, a stranger to much combat with the devil. Wherefore I went to God again, as well as I could, for mercy still. Now also did the tempter begin to mock me in my misery, saying that, seeing I had thus parted with the Lord Jesus, and provoked him to displeasure who would have stood between my soul and the flame of devouring fire, there was now but one way, and that was to pray that God the Father would be a mediator between his Son and me; that he would be reconciled again, and that I might have that blessed benefit in him that his saints enjoyed. Then did that scripture seize upon my soul: "He is of one mind, and who can turn

him?" Oh, I saw it was as easy to persuade him to
make a new covenant or a new Bible besides those we
have already, as to pray for such a thing. This was to
persuade him that what he had done already was mere
folly, and persuade him to alter, yea, to disannul the
whole way of salvation; and then would that saying
rend my soul asunder: "Neither is there salvation in
any other; for there is none other name under heaven
given among men, whereby we must be saved." Acts
4 : 12.

Now the most free and full and gracious words of
the gospel were the greatest torment to me; yea, nothing so afflicted me as the thought of Jesus Christ; the
remembrance of a Saviour, because I had cast him off,
brought forth the villany of my sin and my loss by it to
mind: nothing did twinge my conscience like this; every
thing that I thought of the Lord Jesus, of his grace, love,
goodness, kindness, gentleness, meekness, death, blood,
promises, and blessed exhortations, comforts and conso-
lations, went to my soul like a sword; for still unto
these my considerations of the Lord Jesus, these thoughts
would make place for themselves in my heart: "Aye,
this is the Jesus, the loving Saviour, the Son of God
whom you have parted with, whom you have slighted,
despised, and abused; this is the only Saviour, the only
Redeemer, the only one that could so love sinners as to
wash them from their sins in his own most precious
blood: but you have no part nor lot in this Jesus; you
have put him from you; you have said in your heart,
Let him go if he will. Now therefore you are severed
from him; you have severed yourself from him: behold
then his goodness, but yourself to be no partaker of it."
"Oh," thought I, "what have I lost; what have I parted
with; what has disinherited my poor soul! Oh, it is
sad to be destroyed by the grace and mercy of God—to

have the Lamb, the Saviour, turn lion and destroyer."
Rev. ch. 6. I also trembled, as I have said, at the sight
of the saints of God, especially at those that greatly
loved him, and that made it their business to walk continually with him in this world; for they did, both in
their words, their carriage, and all their expressions of
tenderness and fear to sin against their precious Saviour,
condemn, lay guilt upon, and also add continual affliction and shame unto my soul. The dread of them was
upon me, and I trembled at God's Samuel. 1 Sam.
16 .

CHAPTER VIII

Now also the tempter began afresh to mock my soul another way, saying that "Christ indeed did pity my case, and was sorry for my loss : but forasmuch as I had sinned and transgressed as I had done, he could by no means help me, nor save me from what I feared ; for my sin was not of the nature of theirs for whom he bled and died, neither was it counted with those that were laid to his charge when he hung on the tree. Therefore, unless he should come down from heaven and die anew for this sin, though indeed he did greatly pity me, yet I could have no benefit of him." These things may seem ridiculous to others, even as ridiculous as they were in themselves ; but to me they were most tormenting cogitations : every one of them augmented my misery, that Jesus Christ should have so much love as to pity me when yet he could not help me too ; nor did I think that the reason why he could not help me was because his merits were weak, or his grace and salvation spent on others already, but because his faithfulness to his threatenings would not let him extend his mercy to me. Besides, I thought, as I have already hinted, that my sin was not within the bounds of that pardon that was wrapped up in a promise ; and if not, then I knew surely that it was more easy for heaven and earth to pass away than for me to have eternal life. So that the ground of all these fears of mine did arise from a steadfast belief I had of the stability of the holy word of God, and also from my being misinformed of the nature of my sin. But Oh, how this would add to my affliction, to conceive that I should be guilty of such a sin, for which he did not die. These thoughts did so confound me, and imprison me,

and tie me up from faith, that I knew not what to do.
But Oh, thought I, that he would come down again! Oh
that the work of man's redemption was yet to be done
by Christ; how would I pray him and entreat him to
count and reckon this sin among the rest for which he
died. But this scripture would strike me down as dead:
"Christ being raised from the dead, dieth no more; death
hath no more dominion over him." Rom. 6 : 9. Thus by
the strange and unusual assaults of the tempter my soul
was like a broken vessel, driven as with the winds, and
tossed sometimes headlong into despair; sometimes upon
the covenant of works, and sometimes to wish that the
new covenant and the conditions thereof might, so far as
I thought myself concerned, be turned another way and
changed. But in all these I was as those that jostle
against the rocks, more broken, scattered, and rent.

Oh, the unthought-of imaginations, frights, fears, and
terrors that are effected by a thorough application of
guilt yielding to desperation! This is as the man that
hath his dwelling among the tombs with the dead, who
is always crying out and cutting himself with stones.
Mark 5 : 2–5. But, I say, all in vain; desperation will
not comfort him, the old covenant will not save him.
Nay, heaven and earth shall pass away before one jot or
tittle of the word and law of grace will fail or be removed. This I saw, this I felt, under this I groaned; yet
this advantage I got thereby, namely, a farther confirmation of the certainty of the way of salvation, and
that the Scriptures were the word of God. Oh, I cannot
now express what I then saw and felt of the steadiness
of Jesus Christ, the Rock of man's salvation. What
was done could not be undone, added to, nor altered. I
saw indeed that sin might drive the soul beyond Christ,
even the sin which is unpardonable; but woe to him
that was so driven, for the word would shut him out.

Thus was I always sinking, whatever I did think or do. So one day I walked to a neighboring town and sat down upon a settee in the street, and fell into a very deep pause about the most fearful state my sin had brought me to ; and after long musing, I lifted up my head, but methought I saw as if the sun that shineth in the heavens did grudge to give light, and as if the very stones in the street and tiles upon the houses did bend themselves against me. Methought that they all combined together to banish me out of the world. I was abhorred of them, and unfit to dwell among them, or be partaker of their benefits, because I had sinned against the Saviour. Oh, how happy now was every creature to what I was ; for they stood fast and kept their station, but I was gone and lost.

Then breaking out in the bitterness of my soul, I said to my soul with a grievous sigh, How can God comfort such a wretch ? I had no sooner said it but this returned upon me as an echo doth answer a voice, "This sin is not unto death." At which I was as if I had been raised out of the grave, and cried out again, Lord, how couldst thou find out such a word as this? for I was filled with admiration at the fitness and at the unexpectedness of the sentence—the fitness of the word, the rightness of the timing of it ; the power and sweetness and light and glory that came with it also were marvellous to me to find. I was now for the time out of doubt as to that about which I was so much in doubt before : my fears before were that my sin was not pardonable, and so that I had no right to pray, to repent, etc. ; or that if I did, it would be of no advantage or profit to me. But now, thought I, if this sin is not unto death, then it is pardonable ; therefore from this I have encouragement to come to God by Christ for mercy—to consider the promise of forgiveness as that which stands with open arms to receive me as well as others. This therefore was a great easement to my mind, to wit, that my sin was pardonable—that it was not the sin unto death. 1 John 5 : 16, 17. None but those that know what my trouble was by their own experience, can tell what relief came to my soul by this consideration; it was a release to me from my former bonds, and a shelter from my former storms. I seemed now to stand upon the same ground with other sinners, and to have as good right to the word and prayer as any of them.

Now, I say, I was in hopes that my sin was not unpardonable, but that there might be hope for me to obtain forgiveness. But Oh, how Satan did now lay about him for to bring me down again. But he could by no means do it, neither this day nor the most part of the next, for that sentence, "This sin is not unto death," stood like a mill-post at my back; yet towards the evening of the next day I felt this word begin to leave me, and to withdraw its support from me ; and so I returned to my old fears again, but with a great deal of grudging and peevishness, for I feared the sorrow of despair; nor could my faith long retain this word. But the next day at evening, being under many fears, I went to seek the Lord, and as I prayed I cried, and my soul cried to him in these words with strong cries: "O Lord, I beseech thee show me that thou hast loved me with an everlasting love." I had no sooner said it than with sweetness this returned upon me as an echo or sounding again: "I have loved thee with an everlasting love." Jer. 31 : 3. Now I went to bed in quiet; also, when awakened the next morning, it was fresh upon my soul, and I believed it. But yet the tempter left me not, for it could not be so little as a hundred times that he that day did labor to break my peace. Oh the combats and conflicts that I did then meet with. As I strove to hold by this word,

that of Esau would fly in my face like lightning. I
would be sometimes up and down twenty times in an
hour; yet God did bear me out and keep my heart upon
this word, from which I had also, for several days together, very much sweetness and comfortable hopes of pardon; for thus it was made unto me : "I loved thee while
thou wast committing this sin. I loved thee before, I
love thee still, and I will love thee for ever."

Yet I saw my sin most barbarous, and a filthy crime,
and could not but conclude, with great shame and astonishment, that I had horribly abused the holy Son of God;
wherefore I felt my soul greatly to love and pity him,
and my bowels to yearn towards him, for I saw he was
still my friend, and did reward me good for evil; yea,
the love and affection that then did burn within me to
my Lord and Saviour Jesus Christ, did work at this
time such a strong and hot desire of revenge upon myself, for the abuse I had done unto him, that, to speak as
I then thought, had I a thousand gallons of blood within
my veins, I could freely then have spilled it all at the
command and feet of this my Lord and Saviour.

And as I was thus musing, and in my studies considering how to love the Lord, and to express my love to
him, that saying came in upon me : "If thou, Lord,
shouldest mark iniquities, O Lord, who shall stand?
But there is forgiveness with thee, that thou mayest be
feared." Psa. 130 : 3, 4. These were good words to
me, especially the latter part thereof, to wit, that there
is forgiveness with the Lord, that he might be feared—
that is, as I then understood it, that he might be loved
and had in reverence; for it was thus made out to me:
that "the great God did set so high an esteem upon the
love of his poor creatures, that rather than he would go
without their love, he would pardon their transgressions."
And now was that word fulfilled on me, and I was also

refreshed by it : "Then shalt thou remember, and be confounded, and never open thy mouth any more because of
thy shame, when I am pacified towards thee for all that
thou hast done, saith the Lord God." Ezek. 16 : 63.

Thus was my soul at this time, and as I then did
think, for ever set at liberty from being afflicted with my
former guilt and amazement. But before many weeks
were gone I began to despond again, fearing lest, notwithstanding all I had enjoyed, I might be deserted and
destroyed at the last ; for this consideration came strong
into my mind : that "whatever comfort and peace I
thought I might have from the word of the promise of
life, yet unless there could be found in my refreshment a
concurrence and agreement with the Scriptures, let me
think what I will thereof, and hold it never so fast, I
should find no such thing at the end, for the Scripture
cannot be broken." John 10 : 35. Now began my heart
again to ache and fear I might meet with disappointment
at last. Wherefore I began with all seriousness to ex-
amine my former comfort, and to consider whether one
that had sinned as I had done, might with confidence
trust upon the faithfulness of God laid down in these
words by which I had been comforted, and on which I
had leaned myself.

But now were brought to my mind, " For it is impossible for those who were once enlightened, and have
tasted of the heavenly gift, and were made partakers of
the Holy Ghost, and have tasted the good word of God,
and the powers of the world to come, if they shall fall
away, to renew them again unto repentance." "For if
we sin wilfully after that we have received the knowledge of the truth, there remaineth no more sacrifice for
sins, but a certain fearful looking for of judgment and
fiery indignation, which shall devour the adversaries."
Even "as Esau, who for one morsel of meat sold his birth-

right. For ye know how that afterwards, when he would
have inherited the blessing, he was rejected ; for he found
no place of repentance, though he sought it carefully
with tears." Heb. 6 : 4–6 ; 10 : 27 ; 12 : 17.

Now was the word of the gospel forced from my soul,
so that no promise or encouragement was to be found in
the Bible for me ; and now would that saying work upon
my spirit to afflict me : "Rejoice not, O Israel, for joy,
as other people." Hos. 9 : 1. For I saw indeed there
was cause of rejoicing for those that held to Jesus ; but
for me, I had cut myself off by my transgressions, and
left myself neither foothold nor handhold among all the
stays and props in the precious word of life. And truly
I did now feel myself to sink into a gulf, as a house
whose foundation is destroyed : I did liken myself in
this condition unto the case of a child that was fallen
into a mill-pit, who, though it could make some shift to
scramble and sprawl in the water, yet, because it could
find hold neither for hand nor foot, therefore at last it
must die in that condition. So soon as this fresh assault
had fastened on my soul, that scripture came into my
heart : "This for many days ;" and indeed I found it was
so, for I could not be delivered nor brought to peace
again until well-nigh two years and a half were com-
pletely finished. Wherefore these words, though in
themselves they tended to no discouragement, yet to me,
who feared this condition would be eternal, they were
at some times as a help and a refreshment to me : for,
thought I, many days are not for ever—many days will
have an end ; therefore, seeing I was to be afflicted not
a few, but many days, yet I was glad it was but for
many days. Thus, I say, I would recall myself sometimes, and give myself a help ; for as soon as ever the
word came into my mind, at first I knew my trouble
would be long ; yet this would be but sometimes. for I

could not always think on this, nor even be helped by it, though I did.

Now while the Scriptures lay before me and laid sin anew at my door, that saying in Luke 18:1, with others, did encourage me to prayer. Then the tempter again laid at me very sore, suggesting that neither the mercy of God nor yet the blood of Christ did at all concern me, nor could they help me for my sin; therefore it was but in vain to pray. Yet, thought I, I will pray. But, said the tempter, your sin is unpardonable. Well, said I, I will pray. It is to no boot, said he. Yet, said I, I will pray. So I went to prayer to God; and while I was at prayer, I uttered words to this effect: "Lord, Satan tells me that neither thy mercy nor Christ's blood is sufficient to save my soul. Lord, shall I honor thee most by believing thou wilt and canst; or him, by believing thou neither wilt nor canst? Lord, I would fain honor thee by believing thou wilt and canst." And as I was thus before the Lord, that scripture fastened on my heart, "O man, great is thy faith," even as if one had clapped me on the back as I was on my knees before God; yet I was not able to believe this, that this was a prayer of faith, till almost six months after, for I could not think that I had faith, or that there should be a word for me to act faith on; therefore I would still be as sticking in the jaws of desperation, and went mourning up and down in a sad condition.

There was nothing now that I longed for more than to be put out of doubt as to this thing in question, and as I was vehemently desiring to know if there was indeed hope for me, these words came rolling into my mind: "Will the Lord cast off for ever? and will he be favorable no more? Is his mercy clean gone for ever? doth his promise fail for evermore? Hath God forgotten to be gracious? hath he in anger shut up his tender mer-

cies?" Psa. 77 : 7-9. And all the while they ran in my
mind, methought I had still this as the answer : It is a
question whether he hath or no ; it may be he hath not.
Yea, the interrogatory seemed to me to carry in it a sure
affirmation that indeed he had not, nor would so cast off,
but would be favorable ; that his promise doth not fail,
and that he hath not forgotten to be gracious, nor would
in anger shut up his tender mercy. Something also there
was upon my heart at the same time, which I cannot
now call to mind, with which this text did sweeten my
heart, and make me conclude that his mercy might not
be quite gone, nor gone for ever.

At another time I remember I was again much under
this question, whether the blood of Christ was sufficient
to save my soul ; in which doubt I continued from morning till about seven or eight at night ; and at last, when
I was as it were quite worn out with fear lest it should
not lay hold on me, these words did sound suddenly within my heart, "He is able." But methought this word *able*
was spoke loud unto me ; it showed a great word ; it
seemed to be writ in great letters, and gave such a jostle to my fear and doubt—I mean for the time it tarried
with me, which was about a day—as I had never had
from that all my life, either before or after. Heb. 7 : 25.

But one morning, as I was again at prayer, and trembling under the fear of this, that "no word of God could
help me," that piece of a sentence darted in upon me,
"My grace is sufficient." At this methought I felt some
stay, as if there might be hope. But Oh, how good a
thing it is for God to send his word ; for about a fortnight before I was looking on this very place, and then
I thought it could not come near my soul with comfort ;
therefore I threw down my book in a pet ; then I thought
it was not large enough for me ; no, not large enough ;
but now it was as if it had arms of grace so wide that

it could not only enclose me, but many more besides. By these words I was sustained, yet not without exceeding conflicts, for the space of seven or eight weeks, for my peace would be in it and out sometimes twenty times a day—comfort now, and trouble presently ; peace now, and before I could go a furlong, as full of fear and guilt as ever heart could hold ; and this was not only now and then, but my whole seven weeks' experience. For this about the sufficiency of grace, and that of Esau's parting with his birthright, would be like a pair of scales within my mind—sometimes one end would be uppermost, and sometimes again the other, according to which would be my peace or trouble.

Therefore I did still pray to God that he would come in with this scripture more fully on my heart, to wit, that he would help me to apply the whole sentence, for as yet I could not. What he gave me, that I gathered ; but further I could not go ; for as yet it only helped me to hope there might be mercy for me : " My grace is sufficient." And though it came no further, it answered my former question, to wit, that there was hope ; yet, because "for thee" was left out, I was not contented, but prayed to God for that also. Wherefore one day, when I was in a meeting of God's people, full of sadness and terror, for my fears again were strong upon me, and as I was now thinking my soul was never the better, but my case most sad and fearful, these words did with great power suddenly break in upon me : My grace is sufficient for thee, my grace is sufficient for thee, my grace is sufficient for thee, three times together. And Oh, methought that every word was a mighty word unto me, as *my*, and *grace*, and *sufficient*, and *for thee;* they were then, and sometimes are still, far bigger than others be. At which time my understanding was so enlightened that I was as though I had seen the Lord Jesus look down from heaven through the tiles upon me, and direct these words unto me. This sent me mourning home; it broke my heart and filled me full of joy, and laid me low as the dust, only it stayed not long with me, I mean in this glory and refreshing comfort; yet it continued with me for several weeks, and did encourage me to hope. But as soon as that powerful operation of it was taken from my heart, that other about Esau returned upon me as before; so my soul did hang as in a pair of scales again, sometimes up, and sometimes down; now in peace, and anon again in terror.

Thus I went on for many weeks, sometimes comforted and sometimes tormented; and especially sometimes my torment would be very sore, for all those scriptures aforenamed in the Hebrews would be set before me, as the only sentences that would keep me out of heaven. Then, again, I would begin to repent that ever that thought went through me; I would also think thus with myself: "Why, how many scriptures are there against me? There are but three or four; and cannot God miss them, and save me for all of them?" Sometimes, again, I would think, "Oh, if it were not for these three or four words now, how might I be comforted." And I could hardly forbear at sometimes to wish them out of the book. Then methought I would see as if Peter and Paul and John and all the holy writers did look with scorn upon me, and hold me in derision; and as if they had said unto me, "All our words are truth, one of as much force as the other. It is not we that have cut you off, but you have cast away yourself. There is none of our sentences that you must take hold upon but these, and such as these: 'It is impossible.' 'There remains no more sacrifice for sin.' 'And it had been better for them not to have known the will of God, than after they had known it, to turn from the holy commandment delivered unto them.' For 'the Scripture cannot be broken.'" Heb. 6:4; 10:26; 2 Pet. 2:21; John 10:35. These, as the elders of the city of refuge, I saw were to be the judges both of my case and me, while I stood with the avenger of blood at my heels, trembling at their gates for deliverance; also with a thousand fears and mistrusts, I feared that they would shut me out for ever. Josh. 20:3, 4. Thus was I confounded, not knowing what to do, or how to be satisfied in this question, "whether the Scriptures could agree in the salvation of my soul." I quaked at the apostles; I knew their words were true, and that they must stand for ever.

And I remember one day, as I was in divers frames of spirit, and considering that these frames were according to the nature of several scriptures that came in upon my mind, if this of grace, then was I quiet; but if that of Esau, then tormented. Lord, thought I, if both these scriptures should meet in my heart at once, I wonder which of them would get the better of me. So methought I had a longing mind that they might both come together upon me; yea, I desired of God they might. Well, about two or three days after, so they did indeed; they bolted both upon me at a time, and did work and struggle strongly in me for a while; at last that about Esau's birthright began to wax weak and withdraw and vanish, and this about the sufficiency of grace prevailed with peace and joy. And as I was in a muse about this thing, that scripture came in upon me: "Mercy rejoiceth against judgment." Jas. 2:13. This was a wonder to me, yet truly I am apt to think it was of God; for the word of the law and wrath must give place to the word of life and grace, because, though the word of condemnation be glorious, yet the word of life and salvation doth far exceed in glory, 2 Cor. 3:8–11; also that Moses and Elias must both vanish, and leave Christ and his saints alone.

This scripture did also most sweetly visit my soul : "And him that cometh to me I will in no wise cast out." John 6 : 37. Oh the comfort that I found from this word, "in no wise." As if he had said, By no means, for nothing, whatever he hath done. But Satan would greatly labor to pull this promise from me, by telling me that Christ did not mean me and such as I, but sinners of a lower rank, that had not done as I had done. But I would answer him again : "Satan, here is in these words no such exception ; but *him that cometh—him, any him : 'him that cometh to me* I will in no wise cast out.'" And this I well remember still, that of all the slights that Satan used to take this scripture from me, yet he never did so much as put this question : "But do you come aright ?" And I have thought the reason was, because he thought I knew full well what coming aright was, for I saw that to come aright was to come as I was, a vile and ungodly sinner, and so cast myself at the feet of mercy, condemning myself for sin. If ever Satan and I did strive for any word of God in all my life, it was for this good word of Christ ; he at one end, and I at the other. Oh, what work we made ! It was for this in John, I say, that we did so tug and strive : he pulled, and I pulled ; but, God be praised, I overcame him ; I got sweetness from it.

But notwithstanding all these helps and blessed words of grace, yet that of Esau's selling his birthright would still at times distress my conscience ; for though I had been most sweetly comforted, and that but just before, yet when that came into my mind, it would make me fear again ; I could not be quite rid thereof, it would every day be with me. Wherefore now I went another way to work, even to consider the nature of this blasphemous thought ; I mean, if I should take the words at the largest, and give them their own natural force and scope, even every word therein. So when I had thus considered, I found that if they were fairly taken, they would amount to this : that I had freely left the Lord Jesus Christ to his choice, whether he would be my Saviour or no ; for the wicked words were these : Let him go if he will. Then that scripture gave me hope : " I will never leave thee, nor forsake thee." Heb. 13 : 5. O Lord, said I, but I have left thee. Then it answered again, "But I will not leave thee." For this I thanked God also. Yet I was grievously afraid he would, and found it exceeding hard to trust him, seeing I had so offended him. I should have been exceeding glad that this thought had never entered my mind ; for then I thought I could with more ease and freedom in abundance have leaned on his grace. I saw it was with me as it was with Joseph's brethren ; the guilt of their own wickedness did often fill them with fears that their brother would at last despise them. Gen. 45 : 15, 16.

Yet above all the scriptures that I yet did meet with, that in Joshua, ch. 20, was the greatest comfort to me, which speaks of the slayer that was to flee for refuge. And if the avenger of blood pursue the slayer, then they that are the elders of the city of refuge "shall not deliver him into his hands, because he smote his neighbor unwittingly, and hated him not aforetime." Josh. 20 : 5. Oh, blessed be God for this word. I was convinced that I was the slayer, and that the avenger of blood pursued me I felt with great terror ; it only now remained that I inquire whether I have right to enter the city of refuge. So I found that he must not, · " who lay in wait to shed blood." It was not the wilful murderer, but he who unwittingly did it ; he who did it unawares, not out of spite, or grudge, or malice ; he that shed it unwittingly ; even he who did not hate his neighbor before. Wherefore I thought, verily I was the man that must enter, because I had smitten my neighbor "unwittingly, and hated him not aforetime." I hated him not aforetime; no, I prayed unto him, was tender of sinning against him; yea, and against this wicked temptation I had strove for twelve months before; yea, and also when it did pass through my heart, it did it in spite of my teeth. Wherefore I thought I had a right to enter this city; and the elders, which are the apostles, were not to deliver me up. This therefore was great comfort to me, and gave me much ground of hope.

Yet being very critical, for my smart had made me so that I knew not what ground was sure enough to bear me, I had one question that my soul did much desire to be resolved about, and that was, "whether it be possible for any soul that hath sinned the unpardonable sin, yet, after that to receive though but the least true spiritual comfort from God through Christ." The which, after I had much considered, I found the answer was, No, they could not; and that for these reasons: First, because those that have sinned that sin are debarred a share in the blood of Christ; and being shut out of that, they must needs be void of the least ground of hope, and so of spiritual comfort, "for to such there remains no more sacrifice for sin." Secondly, because they are denied a share in the promise of life: they "shall never be forgiven, neither in this world, nor in that which is to come." Thirdly, the Son of God excludes them also from a share in his blessed intercession, being for ever ashamed to own them, both before his holy Father and the blessed angels in heaven. Heb. 10:26; Matt. 12:32; Mark 8:38.

When I had with much deliberation considered of this matter, and could not but conclude that the Lord had comforted me, and that too after this my wicked sin, then methought I durst venture to come nigh unto those

most fearful and terrible scriptures with which all this
while I had been so greatly affrighted, and on which indeed before I durst scarce cast mine eye, yea, had much
ado a hundred times to forbear wishing them out of the
Bible, for I thought they would destroy me ; but now, I
say, I began to take some measure of encouragement to
come close to them, to read them and consider them, and
to weigh their scope and tendency. The which, when I
began to do, I found their visage changed, for they looked not so grimly as before I thought they did. And first
I came to the sixth of Hebrews, yet trembling for fear it
should strike me : which, when I had considered, I found
that the falling there intended was a falling quite away—
that is, as I conceived, a falling from and absolute denying of the gospel, of the remission of sins by Jesus
Christ ; for from them the apostle begins his argument.
Heb. 6 : 4–6. Secondly, I found that this falling away
must be openly, even in the view of the world, even so
as "to put Christ to an open shame." Thirdly, I found
that those he there intended were for ever shut up of
God, in blindness, hardness, and impenitency. "It is impossible they should be renewed again unto repentance."
By all these particulars I found, to God's everlasting
praise, my sin was not the sin in this place intended.

First, I confessed I was fallen, but not fallen away,
that is, from the profession of faith in Jesus unto eternal
life.

Secondly, I confessed that I had put Jesus Christ to
shame by my sin, but not to open shame ; I did not deny
him before men, nor condemn him as a fruitless one before the world.

Thirdly, nor did I find that God had shut me up, or
denied me to come—though I found it hard work indeed
to come—to him by sorrow and repentance. Blessed be
God for unsearchable grace.

Then I considered the words in the tenth chapter of
the Hebrews, and found, 1. That the wilful sin there
mentioned is not every wilful sin, but that which doth
throw off Christ, and then his commandments too. 2.
That it must be done also openly, before two or three
witnesses, to answer that of the law. Heb. 10 : 28.
3. This sin cannot be committed but with great despite
done to the Spirit of grace—despising both the dissua-
sions from that sin and the persuasions to the contrary.
But the Lord knows, though this my sin was devilish,
yet it did not amount to these

And as touching that in the twelfth chapter of the
Hebrews, about Esau's selling his birthright, though
this was that which killed me, and stood like a spear
against me, yet now I did consider, 1. That his was not
a hasty thought against the continual labor of his mind,
but a thought consented to, and put in practice likewise,
and that after some deliberation. Gen. 25 : 34. 2. It
was a public and open action, even before his brother, if
not before many more : this made his sin of a far more
heinous nature than otherwise it would have been. 3.
He continued to slight his birthright : he did eat and
drink, and went his way ; thus Esau despised his birthright : yea, twenty years after, he was found to despise
it still. "And Esau said, I have enough, my brother :
keep that thou hast unto thyself." Gen. 33 : 9.

Now as touching this, that Esau sought a place of
repentance, thus I thought : 1. This was not for the
birthright, but the blessing ; this is clear from the apostle, and is distinguished by Esau himself : he hath taken
away my birthright, that is, formerly, and now he hath
taken away my blessing also. Gen. 27 : 36. 2. Now
this being thus considered, I came again to the apostle
to see what might be the mind of God, in a New Testa-
ment style and sense, concerning Esau's sin ; and so far

as I could conceive, this was the mind of God : that the
birthright signified regeneration, and the blessing the
eternal inheritance ; for so the apostle seems to hint :
" Lest there be any profane person, as Esau, who for one
morsel of meat sold his birthright ;" as if he should say,
that shall cast off all those blessed beginnings of God
that at present are upon him in order to a new birth,
lest they become as Esau, even be rejected afterwards,
when they should inherit the blessing. For many there
are who in the day of grace and mercy despise those
things which are indeed the birthright to heaven, who
yet, when the deciding day appears, will cry as loud as
Esau, " Lord, Lord, open to us ;" but then, as Isaac would
not repent, no more will God the Father, but will say,
" I have blessed these, yea, and they shall be blessed ;"
but as for you, " Depart from me, ye workers of iniquity." Luke 13 : 25-27.

When I had thus considered these scriptures, and
found that thus to understand them was not against, but
according to other scriptures, this still added further to
my encouragement and comfort, and also gave a great
blow to that objection, to wit, that the Scriptures could
not agree in the salvation of my soul. And now remained only the hinder part of the tempest, for the thunder
was gone beyond me, only some drops did still remain
that now and then would fall upon me ; but because my
former frights and anguish were very sore and deep,
therefore it oft befell me still as it befalleth those that
have been scared with fire. I thought every voice was,
Fire, fire ; every little touch would hurt my tender conscience.

But one day as I was passing into the field, and that
too with some dashes on my conscience, fearing lest yet
all was not right, suddenly this sentence fell upon my
soul : Thy righteousness is in heaven. And methought,

withal, I saw with the eyes of my soul Jesus Christ at God's right hand ; there, I say, was my righteousness ; so that wherever I was, or whatever I was doing, God could not say of me, he wants my righteousness, for that was just before him. I also saw, moreover, that it was not my good frame of heart that made my righteousness better, nor yet my bad frame that made my righteousness worse, for my righteousness was Jesus Christ himself, "the same yesterday, to-day, and for ever." Heb. 13 : 8.

Now did my chains fall off my legs indeed. I was loosed from my afflictions and irons ; my temptations also fled away ; so that from that time those dreadful scriptures of God left off to trouble me ; now went I also home rejoicing for the grace and love of God. So when I came home, I looked to see if I could find that sentence, Thy righteousness is in heaven, but could find no such saying ; wherefore my heart began to sink again, only that was brought to my remembrance : " Of him are ye in Christ Jesus, who of God is made unto us wisdom, righteousness, sanctification, and redemption," 1 Cor. 1 : 30 : by this word I saw the other sentence true ; for by this scripture I saw that the man Christ Jesus, as he is distinct from us as touching his bodily presence, so he is our righteousness and sanctification before God.

Here therefore I lived for some time very sweetly at peace with God, through Christ. Oh, methought, Christ, Christ ! there was nothing but Christ that was before my eyes. I was not now only for looking upon this and the other benefits of Christ apart, as of his blood, burial, or resurrection, but considering him as a whole Christ, as he in whom all these and all other his virtues, relations, offices, and operations met together, and that he sat on the right hand of God in heaven. It was glorious to me to see his exaltation, and the worth and prevalency of all

his benefits, and that because now I could look from myself to him, and would reckon that all those graces of
God that now were green on me, were yet but like those
cracked groats and four-pence-half-pennies that rich men
carry in their purses when their gold is in their trunks
at home.   Oh, I saw my gold was in my trunk at home,
in Christ my Lord and Saviour.   Now Christ was all—
all my righteousness, all my sanctification, and all my
redemption.

Further, the Lord did also lead me into the mystery
of union with the Son of God—that I was joined to him,
that I was flesh of his flesh, and bone of his bone; and
now was that a sweet word to me in Ephes. 5 : 30.   By
this also was my faith in him as my righteousness the
more confirmed in me; for if he and I were one, then
his righteousness was mine, his merits mine, his victory
also mine.   Now could I see myself in heaven and earth
at once; in heaven by my Christ, by my head, by my
righteousness and life, though on earth by my body or
person.   Now I saw Christ Jesus was looked upon of
God, and should also be looked upon by us as that common or public person in whom all the whole body of his
elect are always to be considered and reckoned; that we
fulfilled the law by him, died by him, rose from the dead
by him, got the victory over sin, death, the devil, and
hell by him; when he died, we died; and so of his resurrection: "Thy dead men shall live; together with my
dead body shall they rise," saith he.   And again, "After
two days he will revive us; and the third day we shall
live in his sight."   Isa. ch. 26; Hos. 6 : 2.   Which is
now fulfilled by the sitting down of the Son of man on
the right hand of the Majesty in the heavens; according
to that to the Ephesians: He "hath raised us up together,
and made us sit together in heavenly places in Christ
Jesus."   Ephes. 2 : 6.   Ah, these blessed considerations

and scriptures, with many others of like nature, were in those days made to spangle in mine eye ; so that I have cause to say, "Praise ye the Lord God in his sanctuary ; praise him in the firmament of his power. Praise him for his mighty acts ; praise him according to his excellent greatness."   Psa. 150 : 1, 2.

CHAPTER IX

HAVING thus, in few words, given you a taste of the
sorrow and affliction that my soul endured by the guilt
and terror that these my wicked thoughts did lay me
under, and having given you also a touch of my deliverance therefrom, and of the sweet and blessed comfort
that I met with afterwards, which comfort dwelt about
a twelvemonth with my heart, to my unspeakable admiration, I will now, God willing, before I proceed any farther, give you in a word or two what I conceive was the
cause of this temptation, and also after that, what advantage at the last it became unto my soul.

For the causes, I conceive they were principally two,
of which two also I was deeply convinced all the time
this trouble lay upon me. The first was, for that I did
not, when I was delivered from the temptation that went
before, still pray to God to keep me from the temptations that were to come; for though, as I can say in
truth, my soul was much in prayer before this trial seized me, yet when I prayed only, or at the most principally, for the removal of present troubles, and for fresh
discoveries of his love in Christ, which I saw afterwards
was not enough to do, I also should have prayed that
the great God would keep me from the evil that was to
come. Of this I was made deeply sensible by the prayer
of holy David, who, when he was under present mercy,
yet prayed that God would hold him back from sin and
temptation to come; "for then," saith he, "shall I be
upright, and I shall be innocent from the great transgression." Psa. 19 : 13. By this very word was I galled
and condemned quite through this long temptation.

That was also another word that did much condemn

me for my folly in the neglect of this duty: " Let us
therefore come boldly unto the throne of grace, that we
may obtain mercy, and find grace to help in time of
need." Heb. 4 : 16. This I had not done, and therefore
was thus suffered to sin and fall, according to what is
written : "Pray that ye enter not into temptation." And
truly this very thing is to this day of such weight and
awe upon me, that I dare not, when I come before the
Lord, go off my knees until I entreat him for help and
mercy against the temptations that are to come ; and I
do beseech thee, reader, that thou learn to beware of my
negligence by the afflictions that for this thing I did for
days and months and years with sorrow undergo.

Another cause of this temptation was, that I had
tempted God ; and on this manner did I do it : upon a
time my wife was great with child, and before her full
time was come, her pangs, as of a woman in travail,
were fierce and strong upon her, even as she would have
immediately fallen into labor and been delivered of an
untimely birth. Now at this very time it was that I had
been so strongly tempted to question the being of God ;
wherefore, as my wife lay crying by me, I said, but with
all secrecy imaginable, even thinking in my heart,
"Lord, if now thou wilt remove this sad affliction from
my wife, and cause that she be troubled no more therewith this night"—and now were her pangs just upon
her—"then shall I know that thou canst discern the most
secret thoughts of the heart." I had no sooner said it in
my heart but her pangs were taken from her, and she
was cast into a deep sleep, and so continued till morning. At this I greatly marvelled, not knowing what to
think ; but after I had been awake a good while, and
heard her cry no more, I fell asleep also. So when I
awaked in the morning it came upon me again, even
what I had said in my heart the last night, and how the

Lord had showed me that he knew my secret thoughts, which was a great astonishment unto me for several weeks after.

Well, about a year and a half afterwards, that wicked, sinful thought of which I have spoken before went through my wicked heart, "Let Christ go if he will." So when I was fallen under guilt for this, the remembrance of my other thought, and of the effect thereof, would also come upon me with this retort, which also carried rebuke along with it: "Now you may see that God doth know the most secret thoughts of the heart." And with this, that of the passages that were between the Lord and his servant Gideon fell upon my spirit: how because that Gideon tempted God with his fleece, both wet and dry, when he should have believed and ventured upon his words, therefore the Lord did afterwards so try him as to send him against an innumerable company of enemies, and that too, as to outward appearance, without any strength or help. Judg. 7 : 7. Thus he served me, and that justly; for I should have believed his word, and not have put an *if* upon the all-seeingness of God.

And now to show you something of the advantages that I also gained by this temptation; and first, by this I was made continually to possess in my soul a very wonderful sense both of the blessing and glory of God and of his beloved Son. In the temptation that went before, my soul was perplexed with unbelief, blasphemy, hardness of heart, questions about the being of God, Christ, the truth of the word, and certainty of the world to come: I say, then I was greatly assaulted and tormented with atheism; but now the case was otherwise; now was God and Christ continually before my face, though not in a way of comfort, but in a way of exceeding dread and terror. The glory of the holiness of God did at this time break me to pieces, and the bowels and compassion of Christ did break me as on the wheel; for I could not consider him but as a lost and rejected Christ, the remembrance of which was as the continual breaking of my bones.

The Scriptures also were wonderful unto me; I saw that the truth and verity of them were the keys of the kingdom of heaven: those that the Scriptures favor must inherit bliss; but those that they oppose and condemn must perish for evermore. Oh, this word, "for the Scriptures cannot be broken," would rend the caul of my heart; and so would that other: "Whose sins ye remit, they are remitted; but whose sins ye retain, they are retained." Now I saw the apostles to be the elders of the city of refuge. Josh. 20 : 4. Those that they were to receive in, were received to life; but those that they shut out, were to be slain by the avenger of blood. Oh, one sentence of the Scripture did more afflict and terrify my mind—I mean those sentences that stood against me, and sometimes I thought they every one did—more, I say, than an army of forty thousand men that might come against me. Woe be to him against whom the Scriptures bend themselves.

By this temptation I was made to see more into the nature of the promises than ever I had before; for I now lay trembling under the mighty hand of God, continually torn and rent by the thundering of his justice. This made me, with careful heart and watchful eye, with great fearfulness to turn over every leaf, and with much diligence, mixed with trembling, to consider every sentence, together with its natural force and latitude. By this temptation also I was greatly holden off from my former foolish practice of putting by the word of promise when it came into my mind; for now, though I could not draw that comfort and sweetness from the promise which I

had done at other times, yet, like a man sinking, I would
catch at all I saw.   Formerly I thought I might not meddle with the promise unless I felt its comfort ; but now
it was no time thus to do, the avenger of blood too hardly did pursue me.

Now therefore was I glad to catch at that word,
which yet I feared I had no ground or right to own, and
even to leap into the bosom of that promise that yet I
feared did shut its heart against me.   Now also I would
labor to take the word as God hath laid it down, without
restraining the natural force of one syllable thereof.
Oh, what did I see in the blessed sixth chapter of John :
"And him that cometh to me I will in no wise cast out."
John 6 : 37.   Now I began to consider with myself that
God had a bigger mouth to speak with than I had a
heart to conceive with ; I thought also with myself that
he spoke not his words in haste, or in an unadvised heat,
but with infinite wisdom and judgment, and in very
truth and faithfulness.

I would in these days often, in my greatest agonies,
even flounce towards the promise, as the horses do towards sound ground, and yet stick in the mire ; concluding, though as one almost bereft of his wits through
fear, on this will I rest and stay, and leave the fulfilling
of it to the God of heaven that made it.   Oh, many a
pull hath my heart had with Satan for that blessed sixth
chapter of John.   I did not now, as at other times, look
principally for comfort, though Oh how welcome would
it have been unto me ; but now a word, a word to lean a
weary soul upon, that it might not sink for ever, it was
that I hunted for.   Yea, often when I have been looking
to the promise, I have seen as if the Lord would refuse
my soul for ever ; I was often as if I had run upon the
pikes, and as if the Lord had thrust at me to keep me
from him as with a flaming sword   Then would I think

of Esther, who went to petition the king contrary to the
law. I thought also of Benhadad's servants, who went
with ropes upon their heads to their enemies for mercy.
The woman of Canaan also, that would not be daunted,
though called dog by Christ, and the man that went to
borrow bread at midnight, were also great encourage-
ments unto me. Esth. 4 : 16 ; 1 Kings 20 : 31, etc. ; Matt.
15 : 22, etc. ; Luke 11 : 5-8, etc.

I never saw such heights and depths in grace and
love and mercy as I saw after this temptation—great
sins to draw out great grace ; and where guilt is most
terrible and fierce, there the mercy of God in Christ,
when showed to the soul, appears most high and mighty.
When Job had passed through his captivity, he had
twice as much as he had before. Job 42 : 10. Blessed
be God for Jesus Christ our Lord. Many other things I
might here make observation of, but I would be brief,
and therefore shall at this time omit them, and pray God
that my harms may make others fear to offend, lest they
also be made to bear the iron yoke as I did. I had two
or three times, at or about my deliverance from this
temptation, such strange apprehensions of the grace of
God, that I could hardly bear up under it ; it was so
out of measure amazing, when I thought it could reach
me, that I do think if that sense of it had abode long
upon me it would have made me incapable for business.

Now I shall go forward to give you a relation of
other of the Lord's dealings with me at sundry other
seasons, and of the temptations I then did meet withal.
I shall begin with what I met with when first I joined in
fellowship with the people of God in Bedford. After I
had propounded to the church that my desire was to
walk in the order and ordinances of Christ with them,
and was also admitted by them, while I thought of that

blessed ordinance of Christ which was his last supper
with his disciples before his death, that scripture, "Do
this in remembrance of me," Luke 22:19, was made a
very precious word unto me, for by it the Lord did come
down upon my conscience with the discovery of his
death for my sins, and as I then felt, did as if he plunged
me in the virtue of the same. But behold, I had not
been long a partaker at that ordinance, but such fierce
and sad temptation did attend me at all times therein,
both to blaspheme the ordinance and to wish some dead-
ly thing to those that then did eat thereof, that, lest I
should at any time be guilty of consenting to these
wicked and fearful thoughts, I was forced to bend myself all the while to pray to God to keep me from such
blasphemies; and also to cry to God to bless the cup
and bread to them, as it were, from mouth to mouth.
The reason of this temptation, I have thought since,
was because I did not with that reverence that became
me at first approach to partake thereof. Thus I continued for three quarters of a year, and could never have
rest nor ease; but at the last the Lord came in upon my
soul with that same scripture by which my soul was visited before; and after that I have been usually very
well and comfortable in the partaking of that blessed
ordinance, and have, I trust, therein discerned the Lord's
body as broken for my sins, and that his precious blood
hath been shed for my transgressions.

Upon a time I was something inclining to a consump-
tion, wherewith about the spring I was suddenly and
violently seized with much weakness in my outward
man, insomuch that I thought I could not live. Now
began I afresh to give myself up to a serious examina-
tion of my state and condition for the future, and of my
evidences for that blessed world to come; for it hath, I
bless the name of God, been my usual course, as always,

so especially in the day of affliction, to endeavor to keep my interests in the life to come clear before mine eyes. But I had no sooner began to recall to mind my former experience of the goodness of God to my soul, than there came flocking into my mind an innumerable company of my sins and transgressions; among which these were at this time most to my affliction, namely, my deadness, dulness, and coldness in my holy duties; my wanderings of heart, my wearisomeness in all good things, my want of love to God, his ways, and people, with this at the end of all: "Are these the fruits of Christianity? are these tokens of a blessed man?"

At the apprehensions of these things my sickness was doubled upon me, for now I was sick in my inward man, my soul was clogged with guilt; now also were my former experiences of God's goodness to me quite taken out of my mind and hid, as if they had never been or seen. Now was my soul greatly pinched between these two considerations: Live I must not; die I dare not. Now I sunk and fell in my spirit, and was giving up all for lost; but as I was walking up and down my house as a man in a most woful state, that word of God took hold of my heart: "Ye are justified freely by his grace, through the redemption that is in Christ Jesus." Rom. 3:24. But Oh, what a turn it made upon me. Now was I as one awakened out of some troublesome sleep and dream; and listening to this heavenly sentence, I was as if I had heard it thus spoken to me: "Sinner, thou thinkest that because of thy sins and infirmities I cannot save thy soul; but behold, my Son is by me, and upon him I look, and not on thee, and shall deal with thee according as I am pleased with him." At this I was greatly enlightened in my mind, and made to understand that God could justify a sinner at any time; it was but his looking upon Christ,

and imputing his benefits to us, and the work was forthwith done.

And as I was thus in a muse, that scripture also
came with great power upon my spirit : "Not by works
of righteousness that we have done, but according to his
mercy he saved us." 2 Tim. 1 : 9. Now was I got on
high ; I saw myself within the arms of grace and mercy ;
and though I was before afraid to think of a dying hour,
yet now I cried, Let me die ; now death was lovely and
beautiful in my sight, for I saw we shall never live indeed till we be gone to the other world. Oh, methought,
this life is but a slumber in comparison with that above.
At this time also I saw more in these words, "heirs of
God," Rom. 8 : 17, than ever I shall be able to express
while I live in this world. *Heirs of God!* God himself is
the portion of the saints. This I saw and wondered at,
but cannot tell you what I saw.

Again, as I was at another time very ill and weak :
all that time also the tempter did beset me strongly—
for I find he is much for assaulting the soul when it
begins to approach towards the grave ; then is his opportunity—laboring to hide from me my former experience of God's goodness ; also setting before me the terrors of death and the judgment of God, insomuch that at
this time, through my fear of miscarrying for ever, should
I now die, I was as one dead before death came, and was
as if I had felt myself already descending into the pit.
Methought I said, " There is no way, but to hell I must ;"
but behold, just as I was in the midst of those fears,
these words of the angels carrying Lazarus into Abra-
ham's bosom darted in upon me, as if it were said, "So
shall it be with thee when thou shalt leave this world."
This did sweetly revive my spirits, and help me to hope
in God, which, when I had with comfort mused on a
while, that word fell with great weight upon my mind :

"O death, where is thy sting? O grave, where is thy victory?" 1 Cor. 15 : 55. At this I became both well in body and mind at once, for my sickness did presently vanish, and I walked comfortably in my work for God again.

At another time, though just before I was pretty well and savory in my spirit, yet suddenly there fell upon me a great cloud of darkness, which did so hide from me the things of God and Christ that I was as if I had never seen or known them in my life. I was also so overrun in my soul with a senseless, heartless frame of spirit, that I could not feel my soul move or stir after grace and life by Christ ; I was as if my loins were broken, or as if my hands and feet had been tied or bound with chains. At this time also I felt some weakness seize upon my outward man, which made still the other affliction the more heavy and uncomfortable to me.

After I had been in this condition some three or four days, as I was sitting by the fire I suddenly felt this word to sound in my heart, I must go to Jesus. At this my former darkness and atheism fled away, and the blessed things of heaven were set in my view. While I was on this sudden thus overtaken with surprise, "Wife," said I, "is there ever such a scripture, 'I must go to Jesus ?'" She said she could not tell ; therefore I stood musing still, to see if I could remember such a place. I had not sat above two or three minutes but that came bolting in upon me : "And to an innumerable company of angels ;" and withal, the twelfth chapter of Hebrews, about the mount Sion, was set before mine eyes. Then with joy I told my wife, "Oh, now I know, I know." But that night was a good night to me ; I have had but few better : I longed for the company of some of God's people, that I might impart unto them what God had showed me. Christ was a precious Christ to my soul that night; I could scarce lie in my bed for joy and peace and triumph through Christ.

This great glory did not continue upon me until morning, yet the twelfth chapter of the epistle to the Hebrews was a blessed scripture to me for many days together after this. The words are these: "Ye are come unto mount Sion, and unto the city of the living God, the heavenly Jerusalem, and to an innumerable company of angels, to the general assembly and church of the first-born, which are written in heaven, and to God the Judge of all, and to the spirits of just men made perfect, and to Jesus the mediator of the new covenant, and to the blood of sprinkling, that speaketh better things than that of Abel." Through this sentence the Lord led me over and over, first to this word, and then to that, and showed me wonderful glory in every one of them. These words also have oft since that time been great refreshment to my spirit. Blessed be God for having mercy on me.

CHAPTER X

AND now I am speaking of my experience, I will in this place thrust in a word or two concerning my preaching the word, and of God's dealing with me in that particular also. After I had been about five or six years awakened, and been helped myself to see both the want and worth of Jesus Christ our Lord, and also enabled to venture my soul upon him, some of the most able among the saints with us—I say, the most able for judgment and holiness of life as they conceived, did perceive that God had counted me worthy to understand something of his will in his holy and blessed word, and had given me utterance in some measure to express what I saw to others for edification ; therefore they desired me, and that with much earnestness, that I would be willing at some times to take in hand in one of the meetings to speak a word of exhortation unto them. The which, though at the first it did much dash and abash my spirit, yet being still by them desired and entreated, I consented to their requests, and did twice, at two several assemblies, but in private, though with much weakness and infirmity, discover my gifts among them ; at which they not only seemed to be, but did frequently protest as in the sight of the great God they were both affected and comforted ; and gave thanks to the Father of mercies for the grace bestowed on me. After this, sometimes when some of them did go into the country to teach, they would also that I would go with them ; where, though as yet I did not, and durst not make use of my gifts in an open way, yet more privately still, as I came among the good people in those places, I did sometimes speak a word of admonition unto them also ; the which they, as the others, received with rejoicing at the mercy of God to me-ward, professing their souls were edified thereby.

Wherefore, to be brief, at last, being still desired by the church, after some solemn prayer to the Lord, with fasting, I was more particularly called forth and appointed to a more ordinary and public preaching of the word, not only to and among them that believed, but also to offer the gospel to those who had not yet received the faith thereof ; about which time I did evidently find in my mind a secret inclination thereto, though, I bless God, not for a desire of vainglory, for at that time I was most sorely afflicted with the fiery darts of the devil concerning my eternal state.

But yet I could not be content unless I was found in the exercise of my gift, unto which also I was greatly animated, not only by the continual desires of the godly, but also by that saying of Paul to the Corinthians : "I beseech you, brethren, (ye know the household of Stephanas, that it is the first-fruits of Achaia, and that they have addicted themselves to the ministry of the saints,) that ye submit yourselves unto such, and to every one that helpeth with us, and laboreth." 1 Cor. 16 : 15, 16. By this text I was made to see that the Holy Ghost never intended that men who have gifts and abilities should bury them in the earth ; but rather did command and stir up such to the exercise of their gift, and also did commend those that are apt and ready so to do. "They have addicted themselves to the ministry of the saints :" this scripture in these days did continually run in my mind, to encourage me and strengthen me in this my work for God ; I have also been encouraged from several other scriptures and examples of the godly, both specified in the word and in other ancient histories. Acts 8 : 4 ; 18 : 24, 25 ; 1 Pet. 4 : 10 : Rom. 12 : 6 ; and Fox's Acts and Monuments.

Wherefore, though of myself of all the saints the most unworthy, yet I, but with great fear and trembling at the sight of my own weakness, did set upon the work, and did, according to my gifts and the proportion of my faith, preach that blessed gospel that God had showed me in the holy word of truth; which when the country understood, they came in to hear the word by hundreds, and that from all parts, though upon divers and sundry accounts. And I thank God he gave unto me some measure of bowels and pity for their souls, which also did put me forward to labor with great diligence and earnestness to find out such a word as might, if God would bless it, lay hold of and awaken the conscience, in which also the good Lord had respect to the desire of his servant; for I had not preached long before some began to be touched, and be greatly afflicted in their minds at the apprehension of the greatness of their sin and of their need of Jesus Christ.

I first could not believe that God should speak by me to the heart of any man, still counting myself unworthy; yet those who were thus touched would love me and have a particular respect for me: and though I did put it from me that they should be awakened by me, still they would confess it, and affirm it before the saints of God; they would also bless God for me, unworthy wretch that I am, and count me God's instrument that showed to them the way of salvation. Wherefore, seeing them in both their words and deeds to be so constant, and also in their hearts so earnestly pressing after the knowledge of Jesus Christ, rejoicing that ever God did send me where they were, then I began to conclude it might be so, that God had owned in his work such a foolish one as I; and then came that word of God to my heart with much sweet refreshment: "The blessing of them that are ready to perish is como upon me; yea, I caused the widow's heart to sing for joy." Job 29:13. At this therefore I rejoiced; yea, the tears of those whom God did awaken by my preaching would be both solace and encouragement to me. I thought on these sayings: "Who is he that maketh me glad, but the same that is made sorry by me?" and again, "Though I be not an apostle to others, yet doubtless I am unto you; for the seal of my apostleship are ye in the Lord." 2 Cor. 2:2; 1 Cor. 9:2. These things therefore were as another argument unto me that God had called me to, and stood by me in this work.

In my preaching of the word I took special notice of this one thing, namely, that the Lord did lead me to begin where his word begins—with sinners; that is, to condemn all flesh, and to open and allege that the curse of God by the law doth belong to and lay hold on all men as they come into the world, because of sin. Now this part of my work I fulfilled with great earnestness, for the terrors of the law and guilt for my transgressions lay heavy on my conscience; I preached what I felt, what I smartingly did feel, even that under which my poor soul did groan and tremble to astonishment. Indeed, I have been as one sent to them from the dead; I went myself in chains to preach to them in chains, and carried that fire in my own conscience that I persuaded them to be aware of. I can truly say, and that without dissembling, that when I have been to preach I have gone full of guilt and terror, even to the pulpit-door, and there it hath been taken off, and I have been at liberty in my mind until I have done my work; and then immediately, even before I could get down the pulpit stairs, I have been as bad as I was before; yet God carried me on, but surely with a strong hand, for neither guilt nor hell could take me off my work.

Thus I went on for the space of two years, crying

out against men's sins, and their fearful state because of
them; after which the Lord came in upon my soul with
some sure peace and comfort through Christ, for he did
give me many sweet discoveries of his blessed grace
through him; wherefore now I altered in my preaching,
for still I preached what I saw and felt: now therefore
I did much labor to hold forth Jesus Christ in all his
offices, relations, and benefits unto the world, and did
strive also to discover, to condemn, and remove those
false supports and props on which the world doth both
lean, and by them fall and perish. On these things also
I stayed as long as on the other.

After this God led me into something of the mystery
of the union of Christ; wherefore that I discovered and
showed to them also. And when I had travelled through
these three chief points of the word of God, about the
space of five years or more, I was caught in my present
practice and cast into prison, where I have lain above as
long again, to confirm the truth by way of suffering, as
I was before in testifying of it according to the Scriptures in a way of preaching. When I have been preaching, I thank God my heart hath often, all the time of this
and the other exercises, with great earnestness cried to
God that he would make the word effectual to the salvation of souls, still being grieved lest the enemy should
take the word away from the conscience, and so it should
become unfruitful; wherefore I labored so to speak the
word as that thereby, if it were possible, the sin and
person guilty might be particularized by it.

Also, when I have done the exercise, it hath gone to
my heart to think the word should now fall as rain on
stony places, still wishing from my heart, "Oh that they
who have heard me speak this day did but see as I do
what sin, death, hell, and the curse of God are; and also
what the grace and love and mercy of God are, through

Christ, to men in such a case as they are, who are yet estranged from him." And indeed I did often say in my heart before the Lord, that if to be hanged up presently before their eyes would be a means to awaken them and confirm them in the truth, I gladly should consent to it; for I have been in my preaching, especially when I have been engaged in the doctrine of life by Christ without works, as if an angel of God had stood by at my back to encourage me. Oh, it hath been with such power and heavenly evidence upon my own soul while I have been laboring to unfold it, to demonstrate it, and to fasten it upon the consciences of others, that I could not be contented with saying, I believe and am sure; methought I was more than sure, if it be lawful so to express myself, that those things which then I asserted were true.

When I first went to preach the word abroad, the doctors and priests of the country did open wide against me; but I was persuaded of this, not to render railing for railing, but to see how many of these carnal professors I could convince of their miserable state by the law, and of the want and worth of Christ; for, thought I, this shall answer for me in time to come, when they shall be for my hire before their face. Gen. 30 : 33. I never cared to meddle with things that were controverted and in dispute among the saints, especially things of the lowest nature; yet it pleased me much to contend with great earnestness for the word of faith, and remission of sins by the death and sufferings of Jesus; but, I say, as to other things, I would let them alone, because I saw they engendered strife, and because that they neither in doing nor in leaving undone did commend us to God to be his. Besides, I saw my work before me did run into another channel, even to carry an awakening word; to that, therefore, I did stick and adhere. I never endeavored to nor durst make use of other men's lines, Rom

15 : 18, though I condemn not all that do, for I verily
thought and found by experience that what was taught
me by the word and Spirit of Christ could be spoken,
maintained, and stood to by the soundest and best established conscience ; and though I will not now speak all
that I know in this matter, yet my experience hath more
interest in that text of Scripture, Gal. 1 : 11, 12, than
many among men are aware.

If any of those who were awakened by my ministry
did after that fall back, as sometimes too many did, I
can truly say their loss hath been more to me than if my
own children, begotten of my own body, had been going
to their grave. I think verily I may speak it without
offence to the Lord, nothing has gone so near me as that,
unless it was the fear of the loss of the salvation of my
own soul. I have counted as if I had goodly buildings
and lordships in those places where my children were
born. My heart hath been so wrapped up in the glory
of this excellent work, that I counted myself more blessed and honored of God by this, than if he had made me
the emperor of the Christian world, or the lord of all the
glory of the earth without it. Oh these words : " He
that converteth a sinner from the error of his ways doth
save a soul from death." "The fruit of the righteous is
a tree of life ; and he that winneth souls is wise." "They
that be wise shall shine as the brightness of the firmament ; and they that turn many to righteousness, as the
stars for ever and ever." " For what is our hope, or joy,
or crown of rejoicing ? Are not even ye in the presence
of our Lord Jesus Christ at his coming ? For ye are our
glory and joy." These, I say, with many others of a
like nature, have been great refreshments to me. Jas.
5 : 20 ; Prov. 11 : 30 ; Dan. 12 : 3 ; 1 Thess. 2 : 19, 20.

I have observed that where I have had a work to do
for God, I have had first, as it were, the going of God

upon my spirit to desire I might preach there. I have
also observed that such and such souls in particular
have been strongly set upon my heart, and I stirred up
to wish for their salvation; and that those very souls
have after this been given as the fruits of my ministry.
I have observed that a word cast in by the by hath done
more execution in a sermon, than all that was spoken
besides. Sometimes also, when I have thought I did no
good, then I did most of all; and at other times, when I
thought I should catch them, I have fished for nothing.

I have also observed that where there has been a work
to do upon sinners, there the devil hath begun to roar in
the hearts and by the mouths of his servants; yea, often-
times when the wicked world hath raged most, there have
been souls awakened by the word: I could instance particulars, but I forbear.

My great desire in my fulfilling my ministry was to
get into the darkest places of the country, even among
those people that were farthest off of profession; yet
not because I could not endure the light, for I feared not
to show my gospel to any, but because I found my spirit
did lean most after awakening and converting work, and
the word that I carried did lean itself most that way
also. "Yea, so have I strived to preach the gospel, not
where Christ was named, lest I should build upon another man's foundation." Rom. 15:20.

In my preaching I have really been in pain, and have,
as it were, travailed to bring forth children to God; neither could I be satisfied unless some fruits did appear in
my work. If I were fruitless, it mattered not who com-
mended me; but if I were fruitful, I cared not who did
condemn. I have thought of that: "Lo, children are a
heritage of the Lord; and the fruit of the womb is his
reward. As arrows are in the hand of a mighty man,
so are children of the youth. Happy is the man that

hath his quiver full of them; they shall not be ashamed, but they shall speak with the enemies in the gate." Psa. 127: 3–5. It pleased me nothing to see people drink in my opinions, if they seemed ignorant of Jesus Christ and the worth of their own salvation. Sound conviction for sin, especially for unbelief, and a heart set on fire to be saved by Christ, with strong breathings after a truly sanctified soul, this it was that delighted me; those were the souls I counted blessed.

But in this work, as in all others, I had my temptations attending me, and that of divers kinds; as sometimes I would be assaulted with great discouragement therein, fearing that I should not be able to speak a word at all to edification, nay, that I should not be able to speak sense to the people; at which times I would have such a strange faintness and strengthlessness seize upon my body, that my legs have scarce been able to carry me to the place of exercise.

Sometimes, again, when I have been preaching, I have been violently assaulted with thoughts of blasphemy, and strongly tempted to speak the words with my mouth before the congregation. I have also at times, even when I have begun to speak the word with much clearness, evidence, and liberty of speech, yet been, before the ending of that opportunity, so blinded and so estranged from the things I have been speaking, and have been also so straitened in my speech as to utterance before the people, that I have been as if I had not known or remembered what I have been about, or as if my head had been in a bag all the time of my exercise.

Again, when as sometimes I have been about to preach upon some smart and searching portion of the word, I have found the tempter suggest, "What, will you preach this? This condemns yourself; of this your own soul is guilty; wherefore preach not of this at all, or if you do, yet so mince it as to make way for your own escape; lest, instead of awakening others, you lay that guilt upon your own soul that you will never get from under." But, I thank the Lord, I have been kept from consenting to these so horrid suggestions, and have rather, as Samson, bowed myself with all my might to condemn sin and transgression wherever I found it; yea, though therein also I did bring guilt upon my own conscience. Let me die, thought I, with the Philistines, Judg. 16:30, rather than deal corruptly with the blessed word of God. "Thou that teachest another, teachest thou not thyself?" It is far better then to judge thyself, even by preaching plainly unto others, than that thou, to save thyself, imprison the truth in unrighteousness. Blessed be God for his help also in this.

I have also, while found in this blessed work of Christ, been often tempted to pride and liftings up of heart; and though I dare not say I have not been affected with this, yet truly the Lord of his precious mercy hath so dealt with me, that for the most part I have had but small desire to give way to such a thing; for it hath been my every day's portion to be let into the evil of my own heart, and still made to see such a multitude of corruptions and infirmities therein, that it hath caused hanging down of the head under all my gifts and attainments. I have felt this thorn in the flesh the very mercy of God to me. 2 Cor. 12:8.

I have also had together with this some notable place or other of the word presented before me, which word hath contained in it some sharp and piercing sentence concerning the perishing of the soul, notwithstanding gifts and parts; as for instance, these words have been of great use to me: "Though I speak with the tongues of men and of angels, and have not charity, I am become as sounding brass or a tinkling cymbal." 1 Cor. 13:1.

2. A tinkling cymbal is an instrument of music with which a skilful player can make such melodious and heart-inflaming music, that all who hear him play can scarcely hold from dancing; and yet, behold, the cymbal hath not life, neither comes the music from it, but because of the art of him that plays therewith: so then the instrument at last may come to naught and perish, though in times past such music hath been made upon it. Just thus I saw it was and will be with them that have gifts but want saving grace: they are in the hand of Christ as the cymbal in the hand of David; and as David could with the cymbal make such mirth in the service of God as to elevate the hearts of the worshippers, so Christ can so use these gifted men as with them to affect the souls of his people in the church, yet when he hath done all, lay them by as lifeless though sounding cymbals.

This consideration therefore, together with some others, were for the most part as a maul on the head of pride and desire of vainglory. What, thought I, shall I be proud because I am as sounding brass? Is it so much to be a fiddle? Hath not the least creature that hath life more of God in it than these? Besides, I knew it was love that should never die, but these must cease and vanish; so I concluded a little grace, a little love, a little of the true fear of God, is better than all gifts; yea, and I am fully convinced that it is possible for souls that can scarce give a man an answer but with great confusion as to method—I say, it is as possible for them to have a thousand times more grace, and so to be more in the love and favor of the Lord, than some who by the virtue of the gift of knowledge can deliver themselves like angels.

Thus, therefore, I came to perceive that though gifts in themselves were good to the thing for which they are designed, to wit, the edification of others, yet they are

empty and without power to save the soul of him that
hath them, if they be alone; neither are they as so any
sign of a man's state to be happy, being only a dispensation of God to some, of whose improvement or non-
improvement they must, when a little more time is over,
give an account to Him that is ready to judge the quick
and the dead.   This showed me too, that gifts being
alone were dangerous, not in themselves, but because of
those evils that attend them that have them, to wit,
pride, desire of vainglory, self-conceit, etc., all which
were easily blown up at the applause and commendation
of every unadvised Christian, to the endangering of a
poor creature to fall into the condemnation of the devil.

I saw, therefore, that he that hath gifts had need to
be let into a sight of the nature of them, to wit, that
they come short of making him to be in a truly saved
condition, lest he rest in them, and so fall short of the
grace of God.   He hath cause also to walk humbly with
God and be little in his own eyes, and to remember withal that his gifts are not his own, but the church's, and
that by them he is made a servant to the church; and he
must give at last an account of his stewardship unto the
Lord Jesus; and to give a good account will be a blessed thing.   Let all men therefore prize a little with the
fear of the Lord : gifts indeed are desirable, but yet
great grace and small gifts are better than great gifts
and no grace.   It doth not say the Lord gives gifts and
glory, but the Lord gives grace and glory; and blessed
is such an one to whom the Lord gives grace, true grace,
for that is a certain forerunner of glory.

But when Satan perceived that his thus tempting and
assaulting me would not answer his design, to wit, to
overthrow the ministry and make it ineffectual as to the
ends thereof, then he tried another way, which was to
stir up the minds of the ignorant and malicious to load

me with slanders and reproaches. Now therefore I may say that what the devil could devise and his instruments invent was whirled up and down the country against me, thinking, as I said, that by that means they should make my ministry to be abandoned. It began therefore to be rumored up and down among the people that I was a witch, a Jesuit, a highwayman, and the like. To all which I shall only say, God knows that I am innocent. But as for mine accusers, let them provide themselves to meet me before the tribunal of the Son of God, there to answer for all these things, with all the rest of their iniquities, unless God shall give them repentance for them, for the which I pray with all my heart.

But that which was reported with the boldest confidence was, that I was addicted to gross immoralities and the like. Now these slanders, with the others, I glory in, because but slanders, foolish or knavish lies and falsehoods cast upon me by the devil and his seed; and should I not be dealt with thus wickedly by the world, I should want one sign of a saint and a child of God. "Blessed are ye," saith the Lord Jesus, "when men shall revile you, and persecute you, and shall say all manner of evil against you falsely, for my sake. Rejoice, and be exceeding glad; for great is your reward in heaven: for so persecuted they the prophets which were before you." Matt. 5 : 11, 12.

These things therefore upon mine own account trouble me not; no, though they were twenty times more than they are. I have a good conscience; and whereas they speak evil of me as an evil-doer, they shall be ashamed that falsely accuse my good conversation in Christ. So then, what shall I say to those who have thus bespattered me? Shall I threaten them; shall I chide them; shall I flatter them; shall I entreat them to hold their tongues? No, not I. Were it not that these things make them who are the authors and abettors ripe for damnation, I would say unto them, Report it, because it will increase my glory. Therefore I bind these lies and slanders to me as an ornament; it belongs to my Christian profession to be vilified, slandered, reproached, and reviled; and since all this is nothing else, as my God and my conscience do bear me witness, I rejoice in reproaches for Christ's sake.

I also call upon all those fools and knaves that have thus made it any thing of their business to affirm any of these things aforenamed of me, namely, that I have been of unchaste life or the like, when they have used the utmost of their endeavors and made the fullest inquiry that they can, to prove against me truly that there is any one in heaven, or earth, or hell that can say I have at any time, in any place, by day or night, so much as attempted any unbecoming familiarity. And speak I thus to beg mine enemies into a good esteem of me? No, not I; I will in this beg belief of no man: believe or disbelieve me in this, all is a similar case to me. My foes have missed their mark in this their shooting at me. I am not the man. I wish that they themselves be guiltless. If all the fornicators and adulterers in England were hanged up by the neck till they be dead, John Bunyan, the object of their envy, would be still alive and well. I know not whether there be such a thing as a woman breathing under the cope of the heaven but by their apparel, their children, or by common fame, except my wife.

And in this I admire the wisdom of God, that he made me in this respect circumspect from my first conversion until now. They know and can also bear me witness with whom I have been most intimately concerned, that it is a rare thing to see me to behave familiarly towards females; the common salutation I abhor—it is odious to me in whomsoever I see it. Their company alone I cannot approve, for I think these things are not so becoming me. When I have seen good men salute those women that they have visited, or that have visited them, I have at times made my objection against it; and when they have answered that it was but a piece of civility, I have told them it was not a comely sight: some indeed have urged the "holy kiss;" but then I have asked why they have made such exceptions—why they did salute the most handsome, and let the ill-favored go. Thus, how laudable soever such things have been in the eyes of others, they have been unseemly in my sight.

And now for a wind-up in this matter. I call not only on men but angels to prove me guilty of having broken the marriage-covenant; nor am I afraid to do it a second time, knowing that I cannot offend the Lord in such a case to call God for a record upon my soul that in these things I am innocent. Not that I have been thus kept because of any goodness in me more than any other, but God has been merciful to me, and has kept me; to whom I pray that he will keep me still, not only from this, but every evil way and work, and preserve me to his heavenly kingdom. Amen.

Now, as Satan labored by reproaches and slanders to make me vile among my countrymen, that if possible my preaching might be made of none effect, so there was added hereto a long and tedious imprisonment, that thereby I might be frightened from my service for Christ, and the world terrified and made afraid to hear me preach, of which I shall in the next place give you a brief account.

CHAPTER XI

HAVING made profession of the glorious gospel of Christ a long time, and preached the same about five years, I was apprehended at a meeting of good people in the country, among whom, had they let me alone, I should have preached that day, but they took me away from among them, and had me before a justice, who, after I had offered security for my appearing the next sessions, yet committed me because my sureties would not consent to be bound that I should preach no more to the people.

At the sessions after, I was indicted for an upholder and maintainer of unlawful assemblies and conventicles, and for not conforming to the national worship of the church of England; and after some conference there with the justices, they, taking my plain dealing with them for a confession, as they termed it, of the indictment, did sentence me to perpetual banishment because I refused to conform. So being delivered up to the jailer's hand, I was had home to prison, and there have lain now complete for twelve years, waiting to see what God would suffer those men to do with me. In which condition I have continued with much content, through grace, but have met with many turnings and goings upon my heart, both from the Lord, Satan, and my own corruption; by all which—glory be to Jesus Christ—I have also received among many things much conviction, instruction, and understanding, of which at large I shall not here discourse, only give you a hint or two—a word that may stir up the godly to bless God and to pray for me, and also to take encouragement, should the case be their own, not to fear what man can do unto them.

I never had in all my life so great an inlet into the
word of God as now. Those scriptures that I saw nothing in before, were made in this place and state to shine
upon me; Jesus Christ also was never more real and
apparent than now : here I have seen and felt him indeed.
Oh that word, "We have not preached unto you cun-
ningly devised fables ;" and that, "God raised Christ up
from the dead, and gave him glory, that our faith and
hope might be in God," were blessed words unto me in
this imprisoned condition.   2 Pet. 1 : 16 ; 1 Pet. 1 : 21.
These three or four scriptures also have been great
refreshments in this condition to me : John 14 : 1-4 ;
16 : 33 ; Col. 3 : 3, 4 ; Heb. 12 : 22–24. So that sometimes
when I have enjoyed the savor of them I have been able
to laugh at destruction, and to fear neither the horse nor
his rider.

I have had sweet sights of the forgiveness of my
sins in this place, and of my being with Jesus in another
world. Oh the mount Sion, the heavenly Jerusalem, the
innumerable company of angels, and God the Judge of
all, and the spirits of just men made perfect, and Jesus,
have been sweet unto me in this place. I have seen that
here which I am persuaded I shall never while in this
world be able to express : I have seen a truth in this
scripture : "Whom having not seen, ye love ; in whom,
though now ye see him not, yet believing, ye rejoice
with joy unspeakable and full of glory." 1 Pet. 1 : 8. I
never knew what it was for God to stand by me at all
times and at every offer of Satan to afflict me, as I have
found him since I came in hither ; for lo, as fears have
presented themselves, so have supports and encourage-
ments ; yea, when I have started, even as it were at
nothing else but my shadow, yet God, as being very
tender of me, hath not suffered me to be molested, but
would with one scripture or another strengthen me

against all; insomuch that I have often said, were it
lawful I could pray for greater trouble for the greater
comfort's sake. Eccl. 7 : 14 ; 2 Cor. 1 : 5.

Before I came to prison I saw what was coming, and
had especially two considerations warm upon my heart.
The first was, how to be able to encounter death, should
that be here my portion. And for this that scripture
was great information to me, namely, to pray to God
to be "strengthened with all might, according to his
glorious power, unto all patience and long-suffering with
joyfulness." Col. 1 : 11. I could seldom go to prayer
before I was imprisoned, for a year together, but this
sentence or sweet petition would, as it were, thrust itself
into my mind, and persuade me that if ever I would go
through long-suffering, I must have patience, especially
if I would endure it joyfully.

As to the second consideration, that saying was of
great use to me : "But we had the sentence of death in
ourselves, that we should not trust in ourselves, but in
God that raiseth the dead." 2 Cor. 1 : 9. By this scripture I was made to see that if ever I would suffer right-
ly, I must first pass a sentence of death upon every thing
that can be properly called a thing of this life, even to
reckon myself, my wife, my children, my health, my en-
joyment, and all, as dead to me, and myself as dead to
them. The second was, to live upon God that is invisi-
ble, as Paul said in another place ; the way not to faint
is, to "look not at the things which are seen, but at the
things which are not seen ; for the things which are seen
are temporal, but the things which are not seen are eternal." And thus I reasoned with myself : If I provide only
for a prison, then the whip comes at unawares, and so
doth also the pillory. Again, if I only provide for these,
then I am not fit for banishment ; further, if I conclude
that banishment is the worst, then if death comes I am

surprised ; so that I see the best way to go through sufferings is to trust in God through Christ, as touching the
world to come ; and as touching this world, to count the
grave my house, to make my bed in darkness—to say to
corruption, thou art my father, and to the worm, thou
art my mother and sister : that is to familiarize these
things to me.

But notwithstanding these helps, I found myself a
man encompassed with infirmities ; the parting with my
wife and poor children hath often been to me in this
place as pulling the flesh from the bones, and that not
only because I am somewhat too fond of these great mercies, but also because I would have often brought to my
mind the many hardships, miseries, and wants that my
poor family were like to meet with should I be taken
from them, especially my poor blind child, who lay nearer to my heart than all besides.   Oh, the thoughts of the
hardship my poor blind one might undergo would break
my heart to pieces.   Poor child, thought I, what sorrow
art thou like to have for thy portion in this world !
Thou must be beaten, must beg, suffer hunger, cold,
nakedness, and a thousand calamities, though I cannot
now endure the wind should blow upon thee.   But yet,
recalling myself, thought I, I must venture you all with
God, though it goeth to the quick to leave you.   Oh, I
saw in this condition I was as a man who was pulling
down his house upon the head of his wife and children ;
yet, thought I, I must do it, I must do it.   And now I
thought on those two milch kine that were to carry the
ark of God into another country, and to leave their calves
behind them.   1 Sam. 6 : 10.

But that which helped me in this temptation was
divers considerations, of which three in special here I
will name : the first was the consideration of these two
scriptures : "Leave thy fatherless children, I will pre-

serve them alive; and let thy widows trust in me;" and again, "The Lord said, Verily it shall be well with thy remnant; verily I will cause the enemy to entreat thee well in the time of evil, and in the time of affliction." Jer. 49:11; 15:11.

I had also this consideration, that if I should venture all for God, I engaged God to take care of my concerns; but if I forsook him in his ways, for fear of any trouble that should come to me or mine, then I should not only falsify my profession, but should count also that my concerns were not so sure if left at God's feet while I stood to and for his name, as they would be if they were under my own care, though with the denial of the way of God. This was a smarting consideration, and as spurs into my flesh. That scripture also greatly helped it to fasten the more on me, where Christ prays against Judas, that God would disappoint him in his selfish thoughts which moved him to sell his Master. Pray read it soberly: Psalm 109:6, etc.

I had also another consideration, and that was, the dread of the torments of hell, which I was sure they must partake of that for fear of the cross do shrink from their profession of Christ, his words and laws, before the sons of men. I thought also of the glory that he had prepared for those that in faith and love and patience stood to his ways before them. These things, I say, have helped me when the thoughts of the misery that both myself and mine might, for the sake of my profession, be exposed to, have lain pinching on my mind.

When I have indeed conceited that I might be banished for my profession, then I have thought of that scripture: "They were stoned, they were sawn asunder, were tempted, were slain with the sword; they wandered about in sheepskins and goatskins, being destitute, afflicted, tormented, of whom the world was not wor-

thy," Heb. 11 : 37, for all they thought they were too bad
to dwell and abide among them. I have also thought of
that saying, "The Holy Ghost witnesseth in every city
that bonds and afflictions abide me." I have verily
thought that my soul and it have sometimes reasoned
about the sore and sad estate of a banished and exiled
condition—how they were exposed to hunger, to cold, to
perils, to nakedness, to enemies, and a thousand calamities ; and at last, it may be, to die in a ditch, like a poor
and desolate sheep. But I thank God, hitherto I have
not been moved by these most delicate reasonings, but
have rather by them more approved my heart to God.

I was once, above all the rest, in a very sad and low
condition for many weeks ; at which time also, being but
a young prisoner and not acquainted with the laws, I
had this lying upon my spirits, that my imprisonment
might end at the gallows, for aught that I could tell.
Now, therefore, Satan laid hard at me to beat me out of
heart by suggesting thus unto me : "But how if, when
you come indeed to die, you should be in this condition ;
that is, as not to savor the things of God, nor to have
an evidence upon your soul for a better state hereafter ?"
For indeed at this time all the things of God were hid
from my soul. Wherefore, when I at first began to think
of this, it was a great trouble to me, for I thought with
myself that in the condition I now was in I was not fit
to die ; neither did I think I could if I should be called
to it ; besides, I thought with myself, if I should make a
scrambling shift to clamber up the ladder, yet I should,
either with quaking or other symptoms of fainting, give
occasion to the enemy to reproach the way of God and
his people for their timorousness.

This therefore lay with great trouble upon me, for
methought I was ashamed to die with a pale face and
tottering knees in such a case as this. Wherefore I

prayed to God that he would comfort me, and give me strength to do and suffer what he should call me to; yet no comfort appeared, but all continued hid. I was also at this time so really possessed with the thought of death, that oft I was as if I was on the ladder with a rope about my neck; only this was some encouragement to me: I thought I might now have an opportunity to speak my last words unto a multitude which I thought would come to see me die; and, thought I, if it must be so, if God will but convert one soul by my last words, I shall not count my life thrown away nor lost. But yet all the things of God were kept out of my sight, and still the tempter followed me with, "But whither must you go when you die; what will become of you; where will you be found in another world; what evidence have you for heaven and glory and an inheritance among them that are sanctified?" Thus I was tossed for many weeks, and knew not what to do; at last this consideration fell with weight upon me, That it was for the word and way of God that I was in this condition; wherefore I was engaged not to flinch a hair's breadth from it.

I thought also that God might choose whether he would give me comfort now, or at the hour of death; but I might not therefore choose whether I would hold my profession or no. I was bound, but he was free; yea, it was my duty to stand to his word, whether he would ever look upon me or save me at the last: wherefore, thought I, save the point being thus, I am for going on and venturing my eternal state with Christ, whether I have comfort here or no. If God doth not come in, thought I, I will leap off the ladder even blindfold into eternity, sink or swim, come heaven, come hell. Lord Jesus, if thou wilt catch me, do; if not, I will venture all for thy name.

I was no sooner fixed in this resolution, but this word

dropped upon me: "Doth Job serve God for naught?" As if the accuser had said, Lord, Job is no upright man: he serves thee for by-respects: "Hast thou not made a hedge about him," etc. "But put forth now thy hand, and touch all that he hath, and he will curse thee to thy face." How now, thought I; is this the sign of an upright soul, to desire to serve God when all is taken from him? Is he a godly man that will serve God for nothing, rather than give out? Blessed be God, then I hope I have an upright heart, for I am resolved, God giving me strength, never to deny my profession, though I have nothing at all for my pains; and as I was thus considering, that scripture was set before me, Psalm 44:12, etc. Now was my heart full of comfort, for I hoped it was sincere; I would not have been without this trial for much: I am comforted every time I think of it, and I hope I shall bless God for ever for the teachings I have had by it. Many more of the dealings of God towards me I might relate; but these, out of the spoils won in battle, have I dedicated to maintain the house of the Lord. 1 Chron. 26:27.

THE CONCLUSION

1. Of all the temptations that ever I met with in my
life, to question the being of God and the truth of his
gospel is the worst, and the worst to be borne. When
this temptation comes, it takes away my girdle from me,
and removes the foundation from under me. Oh, I have
often thought of that word, "Having your loins girt
about with truth;" and of that, "When the foundations
are destroyed, what can the righteous do?"

2. Sometimes when, after sin committed, I have looked for sore chastisement from the hand of God, the very
next that I have had from him hath been the discovery of
his grace. Sometimes, when I have been comforted, I
have called myself a fool for my so sinking under trouble. And then, again, when I have been cast down, I
thought I was not wise to give such way to comfort,
with such strength and weight have both these been
upon me.

3. I have wondered much at this one thing, that
though God doth visit my soul with never so blessed a
discovery of himself, yet I have found, again, that such
hours have attended me afterwards, that I have been in
my spirit so filled with darkness that I could not so
much as once conceive what that God and that comfort
was with which I have been refreshed.

4. I have sometimes seen more in a line of the Bible
than I could well tell how to stand under; and yet at
another time the whole Bible hath been to me as a dry
stick, or rather, my heart hath been so dead and dry unto
it that I could not conceive the least dram of refreshment, though I have looked it all over.

5. Of all fears, they are the best that are made by

the blood of Christ; and of all joy, that is the sweetest that is mixed with mourning over Christ. Oh, it is a goodly thing to be on our knees, with Christ in our arms, before God. I hope I know something of these things.

6. I find to this day seven abominations in my heart: 1. Inclining to unbelief. 2. Suddenly to forget the love and mercy that Christ manifesteth. 3. A leaning to the works of the law. 4. Wanderings and coldness in prayer. 5. To forget to watch for what I pray for. 6. Apt to murmur because I have no more, and yet ready to abuse what I have. 7. I can do none of those things which God commands me, but my corruptions will thrust in themselves. "When I would do good, evil is present with me."

7. These things I continually see and feel, and am afflicted and oppressed with, yet the wisdom of God doth order them for my good: 1. They make me abhor myself. 2. They keep me from trusting my heart. 3. They convince me of the insufficiency of all inherent righteousness. 4. They show me the necessity of flying to Jesus. 5. They press me to pray unto God. 6. They show me the need I have to watch and be sober; and, 7. Provoke me to pray unto God, through Christ, to help me and carry me through the world.

The Rev. Robert Philip, author of Bunyan's Life and Times, adds the following: Bunyan's liberation from prison was obtained from Charles II. by Whitehead the Quaker. On his release he soon became one of the most popular preachers of the day, and was, if not the chaplain, "the teacher" of Sir John Shorter, the Mayor of London. Southey's Life.

But although free and popular, Bunyan evidently dreaded every new crisis in public affairs. He had rea-

son to do so. Venner's conspiracy had increased the
severity of his first six years' imprisonment. On the
occasion of the fire in London, he was thrown into prison
again. And soon after James II. came to the throne in
1685, Bunyan conveyed the whole of his property to his
wife by a singular deed, which can only be accounted
for by his suspicions of James and Jeffries, and by his
horror at the revocation of the Edict of Nantz. The asy-
lum which the refugees found in England did not prove
to him that he was safe. No wonder ; "Kirke and his
lambs" were abroad, and the Bedford justices still in
power. It was under these circumstances that he divest-
ed himself of all his property, in order to save his family
from want should he again be made a victim. The deed
shows his solicitude for Mrs. Bunyan's comfort and his
confidence in her prudence. And his Elizabeth well de-
served both.

Whatever Bunyan may have feared when he thus disposed of all the little property he had, nothing befell him
under James II. He published "The Pharisee and Pub-
lican" in 1685, the year of the king's accession ; and in
1688, Charles Doe says "he published six books, being
the time of King James II.'s Liberty of Conscience."
This appears from Doe's list. It throws also much light
upon Bunyan's death. Such labor could not fail to sap
his strength, even if he did nothing but carry the six
books through the press, for none of them are small
except the last. "He was seized with a *sweating* distemper," says Doe, "after he published six books, which,
after some weeks, proved his death." The Sketch in the
British Museum states that, "taking a tedious journey
in a slabby rainy day, and returning late to London, he
was entertained by one Mr. Strudwick, a grocer on Snow
hill, with all the kind endearments of a loving friend,
but soon found himself indisposed with a kind of shak-

ing, as it were an ague, which increasing to a fever, he took to his bed, where, growing worse, he found he had not long to last in this world, and therefore prepared himself for another, towards which he had been journeying as a pilgrim and stranger upon earth the prime of his days."

The occasion of his journey to Reading, which has always been called "a labor of love and charity," will now be more interesting than it hitherto has been. It was not undertaken by a man in health, but by an overwrought author sinking under "a sweating distemper." Mr. Ivimey's account of Bunyan's errand being the best, I quote it:

"The last act of his life was a labor of love and charity. A young gentleman, a neighbor of Mr. Bunyan, falling under his father's displeasure, and being much troubled in mind on that account, and also from hearing it was his father's design to disinherit him, or otherwise deprive him of what he had to leave, he pitched upon Mr. Bunyan as a fit man to make way for his submission, and prepare his mind to receive him; which he, being willing to undertake any good office, readily engaged in, and went to Reading, in Bedfordshire, for that purpose. There he so successfully accomplished his design, by using such pressing arguments and reason against anger and passion, and also for love and reconciliation, that the father's heart was softened, and his bowels yearned over his son.

"After Mr Bunyan had disposed every thing in the best manner to promote an accommodation, as he returned to London on horseback, he was overtaken with excessive rains, and coming to his lodgings extremely wet, he fell sick of a violent fever, which he bore with much constancy and patience, and expressed himself as if he wished nothing more than to depart and to be with Christ, considering it as gain, and life only a tedious

delay of expected felicity.   Finding his strength decay,
he settled his worldly affairs as well as the shortness of
the time and the violence of the disorder would permit;
and after an illness of ten days, with unshaken confidence he resigned his soul, on the 31st of August, 1688,
being sixty years of age, into the hand of his most merciful Redeemer, following his Pilgrim from the city of
Destruction to the New Jerusalem, his better part having
been all along there in holy contemplation, pantings, and
breathings after the hidden manna and the water of life."

His tomb is in Bunhill Fields.   His cottage at Elstow, although somewhat modernized, is substantially
as he left it.   His chair, jug, Book of Martyrs, Church
Book, and some other relics, are carefully preserved at
his chapel in Bedford; and best of all, his *catholic spirit*
also is preserved there.